T0209423

CURATED HEALTH TIPS
—AND—
CANCER-FREE HEALING WAYS

Conversations about
health, tips, healing and self care

CONNIE DELLO BUONO

BALBOA.PRESS
A DIVISION OF HAY HOUSE

Balboa Press books may be ordered through booksellers or by contacting:

Balboa Press
A Division of Hay House
1663 Liberty Drive
Bloomington, IN 47403
www.balboapress.com
1 (877) 407-4847

Print information available on the last page.

ISBN: 978-1-9822-4261-9 (sc)
ISBN: 978-1-9822-4262-6 (e)

Balboa Press rev. date: 02/06/2020

CONTENTS

LEARNING HEALING WAYS

Twenty five years ago, I had my first homebirth with midwives in San Jose California. Now, I am training caregivers how to massage seniors who are bed ridden and dying of cancer. I incorporate holistic way of making them feel good or live longer in the last years of their lives with nutrition and other healing ways. Because of my experience as a pharmacy technician instructor, I was able to match the care of each client based on their body and their set of medications.

I brought massage oils with essential oils (eucalyptus, rosemary, ginger, etc) and other home made remedies from ginger tea, hydrogen peroxide for mouth wash and body wash, apple cider vinegar, garlic and baking soda. In all this, I learned that each age, ethnicity, marital status, stress, jobs, exposure to toxins from work and home affect the way we use nutrition, massage and healing ways. With the passing of both my mother and father from liver and lung cancer, I vowed to share with others lessons I learned in the past 40 years which contribute to their health decline.

Cancer started 40 years ago before my mom died at 83. I saw her toxic work environment, invading organisms in the well water, IUD infection and other contributing inflammation and stressors. I now know that cancer started from these stressors, bad microbes, lifestyle, age and inflammation. There are many more root causes and now we can arm ourselves to fight cancer and be cancer-free with a team of caregivers, loving family and friends and health care professionals.

I thank the recent development in research and science and the internet as I scour the net for information. I hope to bring simple easy to understand information to benefit our future generation in the area of home care, cancer, herbs, nutrition, parasites, lifestyle, sleep, exercise and in the way we treat our bodies.

This book list stories, senior home care, causes of cancer and ways to heal our body and the last topic is holistic mother and baby care using herbs and nutrition. Doctors cure and we heal our own bodies if we know how from our grandmothers to current research or just by googling words.

How my grandma self hacked health and healing

At 94 yrs of age, she cannot prolong her life any longer with no nutrition and with heavy work during her lifetime as breadwinner in the family and going to each son or daughter (7 children) and taking care of her grandchildren. But Claudia Defensor Poral showed me healing ways that science can explain now how it promoted health.

- Massaging the inner palm of hands, armpit and inner thighs where the lymph nodes are located. This massage can heal a fever in a shorter period of time and provide relief in many ways.
- Using garlic, ginger and other herbs to include in her massage oil or soups.
- Burning the egg yolk as skin paste to kill fungus and washing with boiled guava leaves.
- Burn the rice as activated charcoal for diarrhea and stomach problems.
- Making other herbal poultice for all kinds of home health remedies.
- Her staple nourishment comes from boiled greens, sweet potatoes, green plantain bananas and boiled eggs.
- For her leg pain, her massage oil is a combo of ginger, garlic, salt and other herbs such as yerba buena, lemongrass and oregano
- She would create a bonfire in the backyard and curse the evil spirits if she thinks they are the cause of a sudden aches and pain of one of her children or their families.

Why have endocrinological diseases like diabetes, thyroiditis become so common these days?

Stress is the answer with most of us not taking a nap and not getting uninterrupted 9 hours sleep. NIH-funded study suggest sleep clears brain of damaging molecules associated with neurodegenation (doi: 10.1126/

science.1241224). Infection-fighting antibodies and cells are reduced during periods when you don't get good night time sleep. When you don't sleep enough, stress response produces chronic low-grade inflammation (Pfluges Arch. 2012 Jan; 463(1):121-137. doi: 10.1007/s00424-011-1044-0).

Adrenals and liver come to the rescue as blood sugar levels drop. A detox of these organs can help fight parasites that causes infections and stress in our bodies. The endocrine pancreas, liver and adrenal glands work to normalize blood sugar and triglycerides. The insulin secreting beta cells of the endocrine pancreas is a target of infection from parasites and other pathogens (Parasitol Res. 2017 Mar; 116(3):827-838 doi:10.1007/s00436-016-5350-5).

The liver seems to be attractive to many parasites (Verh Dtsch Ges Pathol. 1995;79:241-8). If it has parasites, clean or detox your liver first. Parasites, fungus and other pathogens had been detected within adrenal glands. The immune system's ability to fight off antigens is reduced when we are stressed (Kiecolt-Glaser, et al., 1984). Stress is indirectly associated with bad habits.

Take care of your stress so it will be easier for you to prevent obesity, depression, sugar cravings and nerve pain which may start to happen at around 55 years of age. When we take care of our stress level, we take care of our metabolism, brain, whole body and we then prevent chronic diseases that lead to cancer.

Note: Pituitary gland in the brain responsible for stress hormones, sex hormones, sleep and food cravings have been reported to to be infected with amebiasis, malaria, hydatid disease, toxoplasmosis and neurocysticercosis among children (doi: 10.17352/ijchem.000022).

Activities to make you happy

Beach stroll, dancing, watching comedians, laughing, sleeping at night, massage, happy and loving friends and relationships, spending time with family and friends, playing with your pets, gardening, singing, praying, deep breathing exercise, meditation

Anxiety, Autoimmune diseases, Cancer, Chronic fatigue syndrome, Common Colds, Hormone imbalance, Irritable bowel disease, Thyroid conditions, Weight loss resistance

Needed nutrients

Digestive enzymes, vitamin C (citrus, kiwi, berries, tamarind), vitamin B, L-carnitine, chromium, anti-oxidants, fiber-rich foods (squash, yams, sulfur family of garlic and onions, greens, okra, radish), spearmint, ginger, beets, carrots, all root crops, sprouts, pineapple, papaya, taurine rich foods (breastmilk, sea algae, fish)

Adaptogenic herbs

1. Eleuthero ginseng
2. Holy basil
3. Rodiola rosea
4. ashwagandha
5. Astralagus
6. Sour date
7. Mimosa pudica
   Extracts of Mimosa pudica are successful in wiping out harmful bacteria and can be useful in antibacterial products
8. Medicinal mushrooms
   Mushrooms are rich in B vitamins such as riboflavin (B2), folate (B9), thiamine (B1), pantothenic acid (B5), and niacin (B3).
9. Licorice root
10. Valerian

Signs of the preactive and active phase of dying, medications for terminally ill

I was my mom's caregivers for 4 nights and days before cancer enveloped her organs. With her yellow skin and hard tummy, the parasites and cancer are feasting on her liver and nearby organs. Two weeks before she died, her head was so warm and she has difficulty hearing with so many noise in her ears. Hours before her death, I saw blackened spots on her legs. When she died, black and colorless liquid came out of her nose as if her tummy is being emptied. For many nights, she is comatose but can still turn side to side as if she is fighting the parasites and cancer growing. She cannot swallow any more and weeks before her death, she suddenly talk and said hi to her sister who died many years ago.

I witnessed another death as I kept vigil for one of our clients who has cancer. I saw pinpoint pupils the day he died. And in last minute, tears flowing on the side of the eye that was drooping. He was in sleep mode all afternoon that we just monitored his oxygen supply. And then his BP reading was very low and so is the oxygen level. Immediately, coldness covered his face. As we lay him flat on the floor, the paramedics spent 20 min resuscitating him to no avail. The paramedics asked permission for the family to discontinue their efforts after 20 minutes. Silenced emanated the place. I cried, said a prayer with the family and lit incense. It was 8pm.

At around 10am that day, he was still alert swallowing all the medications powdered and added in the apple juice. There was no poop or urine from 12noon to 8pm. When the bite of lunch came, tuna with mayo on crackers, he cannot swallow some of it. The progress was so fast from deep sleep, coma to coldness. And when the oximeter registered at 49, we called 911. He planned his last days in his home, we worked hard to take him out of the hospital IVs and MRI scans and more tests. He died in peace.

Now, I question why the medications were prescribed for a terminally ill patient with MRI scan showing a network of baby strokes to happen soon and the chest with progressing lung cancer. The patient asked for his oxycontin pain med at 3 am. He swallowed two of them. And then had a clear voice talking about his plans for his business.

We gave the meds as prescribed by his hospital since his family is supporting his wishes to live longer. I could oppose the meds to allow his liver cells to recover but I am only the caregiver, assisting the client's daily living and providing comfort that the pain meds cannot offer.

Signs of the preactive phase of dying

- ✓ increased restlessness, confusion, agitation, inability to stay content in one position and insisting on changing positions frequently (exhausting family and caregivers)
- ✓ withdrawal from active participation in social activities
- ✓ increased periods of sleep, lethargy, eyes are closed most of the time
- ✓ decreased intake of food and liquids, difficulty swallowing
- ✓ beginning to show periods of pausing in breathing (apnea) whether awake or sleeping
- ✓ patient reports seeing persons who had already died
- ✓ patient states that he or she is dying, feeling of giving up
- ✓ patient requests family visit to settle "unfinished business" and tie up "loose ends"
- ✓ inability to heal or recover from wounds or infections, feet have dark spots of bruishing
- ✓ increased swelling (edema) of either the extremities or the entire body

Signs of the Active Phase of Dying

- ✓ inability to arouse patient at all (coma) or, ability to only arouse patient with great effort but patient quickly returns to severely unresponsive state (semi-coma)
- ✓ severe agitation in patient, hallucinations, acting "crazy" and not in patient's normal manner or personality, eyes looking upward
- ✓ much longer periods of pausing in breathing (apnea)
- ✓ dramatic changes in the breathing pattern including apnea, but also including very rapid breathing or cyclic changes in the patterns of breathing (such as slow progressing to very fast and then slow again, or shallow progressing to very deep breathing while also changing rate of breathing to very fast and then slow)
- ✓ other very abnormal breathing patterns
- ✓ severely increased respiratory congestion or fluid buildup in lungs

- ✓ inability to swallow any fluids at all (not taking any food by mouth voluntarily as well)
- ✓ patient states that he or she is going to die
- ✓ patient breathing through wide open mouth continuously and no longer can speak even if awake, not responsive
- ✓ urinary or bowel incontinence in a patient who was not incontinent before
- ✓ marked decrease in urine output and darkening color of urine or very abnormal colors (such as red or brown)
- ✓ blood pressure dropping dramatically from patient's normal blood pressure range (more than a 20 or 30 point drop)
- ✓ systolic blood pressure below 70, diastolic blood pressure below 50
- ✓ patient's extremities (such as hands, arms, feet and legs) feel very cold to touch
- ✓ patient complains that his or her legs/feet are numb and cannot be felt at all
- ✓ cyanosis, or a bluish or purple coloring to patients arms and legs, especially the feet, knees, and hands)
- ✓ patient's body is held in rigid unchanging position
- ✓ jaw drop; the patient's jaw is no longer held straight and may drop to the side their head is lying towards

Medications for terminally ill

It is normal and acceptable to remove regular medications during the very end stage of dying, what is called "active phase of dying," since the patient's body will not be benefited by them and all the systems and organs are shutting down and collapsing in the process of death.

At this stage, the patient often has difficulty swallowing, may not absorb the medications due to dehydration as well as liver and other organ failure, and giving the medications may be more troublesome than any benefit they could offer.

At the very end of the active phase of dying, only comfort medications (pain meds) are given so that the patient is allowed to die without suffering. At this point, there is absolutely no way of preventing death anyway, and any of the ordinary routine medications the patient used to take have no medical justification or value.

Ginger - Coffee hot drink

fresh ginger, honey or brown sugar, coffee, water

Instruction

1. Cut fresh ginger in small pieces and let it boil for 5 minutes.
2. Mix hot ginger and coffee in 50:50 proportion.
3. Sweeten with honey or brown sugar or coconut sugar.
4. Serve hot.

Bitter melon and scrambled eggs (blood cleansing, sugar control, fiber-rich)

bitter melon, eggs, tomatoes, onions, garlic, ginger powder, mushrooms

Clean bitter melon by removing the inner seeds and massage with oil and squeezed and then sauteed with garlic, tomatoes, onions, ginger powder and mushrooms. When closed to cooked, add scrambled eggs. Salt to taste. Serve warm.

High blood pressure go to home remedies

Apple cider vinegar, coughing, vitamin C, garlic, warm water, rest, deep breathing

Story

Our senior client who is bedridden and terminally ill loves this coffee ginger mix. Ginger cleans the blood while coffee is a stimulant. Use decaf or diluted coffee if there is heart issues. Only drink a cup in the morning with protein rich breakfast of egg (soft boiled). You can use ginger powder.

Why write an ebook about cancer?

After the loss of my parents from lung and liver cancer, I wanted to understand about lifestyle and environment that contributes to the progression of cancer. In the process, it helps me grieve and give back to others and learn from these events. Journaling is therapeutic. Writing about health and cancer is my way of giving back to others about my experience in the area of health, cancer, and caregiving.

When my father died of lung cancer and my mother of liver cancer, I vowed to educate the public of cancer signs and train my caregivers and clients about preventive care. As a former pharmacy tech instructor, I learned about our medicines. Antibiotics work and so are some medicines. We need surgery to remove tumors since our liver can regenerate if we are still young.

We made mistakes with regards to the use of some drugs, especially with seniors. You can tell from their bruised skin that the acidic meds are breaking off the already fragile small capillaries and other blood vessels.

There are winners in the home health care and cancer area. One of them is my client with interstitial lung disease and cancer. His doctors told him that he has only 6 months to live and with our home care with caring caregivers, he lived for more than 16 months and still is living today.

We use massage and healthy soups of sulfur rich veggies such as garlic and onions. He used his knowledge about health as a former firefighter in Palo Alto. He used his mind power, even when his hospital Kaiser dismissed his case as terminal.

He drinks his warm tea, protein shake, moves around with his prosthetics, massages his legs and measures his oxygen level many times during the day with his pulse oximeter.

The other winner is me. I have no medical insurance for many years and I delivered my children at home with nurse midwives more than 20 years ago. I know that I have to monitor my health and own it. With fast heart beat, the doctor said I can have surgery or just cough. I chose to cough and use preventive healing ways. I believe I have ingested or growing some bugs/toxins, thus the tachycardia. I asked my dentist to replace my metal fillings but he did not remove all. I am taking activated charcoal, digestive enzymes, and other anti-parasitic meds to detox.

Each time I visit a house of a senior needing home care, I inspect the canned foods in the kitchen, absence of filtered water, mold in the house, color of her/his feet and softness or hardness of her/his stomach. Death approaches when there are black spots on the feet and the stomach is hard.

I always asked the caregiver for night shift to hold the client's hands, use some massage oil (mixed with essential oils of eucalyptus and rosemary), pray with them and cheer them up.

I collected many health related answers from various sources including the internet and I posted at quora.com and clubalthea.com that I am now collecting all my posts in an ebook format. 20% of the profit will go to college funds of aspiring students and for affordable senior care and housing. The ebook will be free to all libraries and senior community centers.

Get your blood tests done regularly. When I told my mother's doctor about the elevated liver enzymes in my mom's blood test, she brushed it off as just my mom needing to rest more from working as a caregiver and to drink less alcohol. She died a few years later of liver cancer.

Lung cancer cannot be detected without using an MRI and CAT scan. So when my father found out about his lung cancer diagnosis from the scans, he hid it from the family. He just arrived in California and does not want to die early and go home. He fought for 9 months with massage and juice from green papaya and apples.

My mother's low platelet count and knee pain were observed for many months and many years before, she had complained of skin itching and pain in her abdomen.

She doesn't want to be bed ridden. She fought for 2 weeks on the bed before she succumb to liver cancer.

I have taught bay area seniors about preventive health and taught caregivers about use of massage, healthy meals and holistic senior care. I learned from my mother who was a caregiver for 18 years and my grandma, Claudia, who used massage and herbs to heal us when we were young.

Many of my relatives died of heart disease. I suspect our family has an iron metabolism dysfunction. But now, there are many ways to learn about health and identify our chronic disease before it progresses from tumor markers to other biomarkers.

Thanks to the many scientists, geneticists, and health care team who bring health care and health care solutions to this century.

How my mom lived 40 more years before liver cancer stopped her?

Forty years ago, my mom had a hysterectomy to remove the tumors from her ovaries and uterus. It started with an infected tube from an IUD, bacteria and other invading pathogens in our water and exposure to chemicals in the garment factory where she worked. She is also lacking in sleep raising 6 children.

During the last 18 years of her life, she lived in San Jose, California. Every Sunday, I would bring a big bag of produce from the farmer's market. And we go to the Asian supermarket for her fish, shrimp and beef bones. I supply her with vitamins and massage oil from whole foods.

She adds ginger in her massage oil and boils ginger for her own anti-flu warm drink. She discovered red wine and has been addicted to it and drinks only at night with her boiled eggs or dumplings. She loves dried salted fish.

During the last 2 months, she can feel that the tumor is growing and said goodbye to us and happy knowing that most of her grandchildren completed college because of her financial support.

During the times that she has aches and pain, she would massage herself. She loves her garden. She loves her friends. She always get sick when she goes home to the Philippines. Four years before she died, she can feel that she is gasping for breath, had lost her appetite and has difficulty swallowing. On two occasions, she cannot walk that her knee must be suctioned from the growing pus inside. Her skin is always itchy and had back pain too.

She cannot see herself retiring that she worked until she was 82 years of age. She is remembered as a generous grandma, loyal to her family and very friendly to all. She cooked for strangers and has a happy laugh all the time even when she is tired.

About my father's lung cancer

He was born as the third son in the family, my grandma did not breastfeed him. He started smoking at age 19. And worked as a security guard and mechanic at a mining company of copper and nickel. He moved from one island to another and finally settled in one of the slums of Manila with his 6 children. He worked non-stop as a limo driver, driving 24-hours non-stop at one time, as a result he suffered from Tuberculosis. He took meds for his TB and hepatitis.

Before he died at 64, he stopped smoking (cold turkey). He loved to eat burned BBQ of chicken feet and meat.

His lung cancer was diagnosed after a CAT scan and MRI scan. His doctors said that he has 3 months to live and he survived for 10 more months with green papaya juice, protein smoothie and massage. We used oxygen tanks for him and forgot to add a painkiller in his regimen. He said that the pain is like hell while he is still on earth. He died at home surrounded by family.

Air pollution in the Philippines

I always came home with dark soot inside my nose when I was in college commuting to the city of Manila, an hour away from Bacoor, Cavite. There is no regulation for drivers to pass smog test before they can drive their vehicles. Some tourists find the city of Manila to be very smoggy city when compared to other countries.

Indoor contaminants include: particulate matter, carbon monoxide, secondhand tobacco smoke, pesticides, solvents, volatile organic compounds, biological pollutants: mites/allergens/moulds, built environment, radon, asbestos, occupation-related contaminants.

Current News

Emphysema is considered a smoker's disease. But it turns out, exposure to air pollution may lead to the same changes in the lung that give rise to emphysema.

A new study published Tuesday in JAMA finds that long-term exposure to slightly elevated levels of air pollution can be linked to accelerated development of lung damage, even among people who have never smoked.

The study looked at the health effects of breathing in various pollutants, including ground-level ozone, the main component of smog.

The researchers found that people in the study who were exposed for years to higher-than-average concentrations of ground-level ozone developed changes to their lungs similar to those seen in smokers.

Ways to cut air pollution

- Cloud Seeding
- Giant Sprinklers
- Smog-Eating Buildings
- Pigeon Air Patrol
- Smog Free Tower
- All Electric: Setting the Stage For Zero-Emissions Vehicles
- City Tree: Purifying Urban Areas the Natural Way
- Fuel Bans: Taking Fossil Fuels Off the Roads For Good
- Pollution Vacuum Cleaners: Sucking Up the Air's Contaminants
- Require all students to plant trees before graduating in high school or elementary

ABOUT CANCER, WHAT CAN YOU DO ABOUT IT?

Cancer cells are abnormal and take over your normal cell functions and will deplete your body with important nutrients. Sounds like parasites, molds, fungus and other microbes inhabiting us and all of a sudden becomes our enemies devouring our good cells. When a death occurs, they come out as black matter from liquid running out our nose or our fecal matter mixed with blood and debris of cancer cells, black.

Before cancer can multiply, there are signs that you can notice many years before from chronic lack of sleep, chronic pain, chronic fatigue, chronic bloating or metabolic disorders, chronic cough and loss of appetite or loss of weight. The knee weakens, fast heart beat is felt, difficulty breathing, inability to sleep at night, low energy during day time, irritability and sensitive to light, noise, temperature and heat.

What can you do about it? Stay away from cancer-causing fumes, molds, fungus, toxic metals, toxic foods (3-day old rice, dried salted fish, farmed food products, moldy and expired foods, processed foods), cancer-causing or hormone-disrupting chemicals from hormones fed in cows, plastics, and other carcinogens from burnt BBQ meat and others you can easily notice since they are not whole foods but processed and they can make you ill, nauseous and gives you tummy or headache.

So what else can we do about cancer, you can slowly detox your body from these toxins with sleep, clean air, and water, whole foods, exercise, sunshine and avoidance of these toxins (parasites, left overs, molds, fungus, metal toxins in dentures and from the environment).

Step 1 to cancer free: Limit stress that leads to high blood glucose and lipids

Adrenals and liver come to the rescue as blood sugar levels drop. The endocrine pancreas, liver and adrenal glands work to normalize blood sugar and triglycerides.

Take care of your stress so it will be easier for you to prevent obesity, depression, sugar cravings and nerve pain which may start to happen at around 55 years of age. When we take care of our stress level, we take care of our metabolism, brain, whole body and we then prevent chronic diseases that lead to cancer.

Activities to make you happy: beach stroll, dancing, watching comedians, laughing, sleeping at night, massage, happy and loving friends and relationships, spending time with family and friends, playing with your pets, gardening, singing, praying, deep breathing exercises and meditation.

Side effects of chronically elevated cortisol

Anxiety, autoimmune diseases, cancer, chronic fatigue syndrome, common colds, hormone imbalance, irritable bowel disease, thyroid conditions, weight loss resistance

Needed nutrients

Digestive enzymes, vitamin C (citrus, kiwi, berries, tamarind), vitamin B, L-carnitine, chromium, anti-oxidants, fiber-rich foods (squash, yams, sulfur family of garlic and onions, greens, okra, radish), spearmint, ginger, beets, carrots, all root crops, sprouts, pineapple, papaya, taurine rich foods (breastmilk, sea algae, fish)

Adaptogenic herbs

- Ginger
- Eleuthero or panax ginseng
- Holy basil
- Rhodiola Rosea
- ashwagandha

- Astralagus
- Sour date
- Mimosa pudica
- Water Hyssop
- Omija

Extracts of Mimosa pudica are successful in wiping out harmful bacteria and can be useful in antibacterial products.

Medicinal mushrooms are wealthy in B vitamins like vitamin G (B2), vitamin B complex (B9), thiamin (B1), vitamin (B5), and B complex (B3). Licorice root, Valerian

Step 2 to cancer free: Sleep

Adequate sleep at night

Give yourself 1 point if you believe that adequate sleep allows you to fight cancer cells and allows you to detox or cleanse your cells from toxins.

In cold temperature, with less worry and right time each night, with small protein rich food at dinner before 7 pm, allow your body to get rid of toxins by getting adequate sleep. Write a journal or notes to free your mind from worries and constant thoughts and allow your body to rest and relax with a calm mind. It takes 30 minutes to digest eggs (a complete protein) while it takes 4 hours to digest red meat.

Many cancer clients have less than 4 hours of uninterrupted sleep years before they had cancer. And recent research attributes cancer growth to lack of sleep from cancer cells or microbes causing a cancer not allowing the human body to sleep at night.

Step 3 to cancer free: kill bad microbes from environment

The word microbe sounds alarming---we tend to associate them with respiratory illness, ebola, you name it. But microbiologist Dr. Jonathan Eisen has given an illuminating TEDTalk that will make you put down the hand sanitizer.

As Eisen explains, "We are coated in a cloud of microbes, and these microbes have good effects on us rather than killing us." Fun fact about microbes: the typical healthy adult has ten times as several microbe cells as human cells. There are good microbes and invading bad microbes such as parasites, fungus and virus.

Parasites interact with natural and anthropogenic (chiefly of environmental pollution and pollutants) originating in human activity) stressors to increase mortality and reduce animal/human health in myriad ways in a wide spectrum of host and parasite taxa.

The combined effects of parasites and other stressors can reduce either resistance or tolerance to infection.

Good microbes play defense

The stacks of microbes that survive and within the United States of America defend the United States of America from pathogens just by seizing the area. By occupying spots wherever nasties may get access to and thrive, sensible microbes keep the United States of America healthy. As Eisen explains, "It's sort of like how having a nice ground cover around your house can prevent weeds from taking over."

Good microbes boost the immune system

Researchers at Loyola University demonstrated in a 2010 study how Bacillus, a rod-shaped bacteria found in the digestive tract, binds to immune system cells and stimulates them to divide and reproduce. The analysis suggests that, years down the road, those with weakened immune systems could be treated by introducing these bacterial spores into the system. **These microbes could potentially even help the body fight cancerous tumor.**

If the microbiome is thrown out of whack, it can alter the body's ability to differentiate between itself and foreign invaders.

Recent research in Type 1 Diabetes reveals that a disturbance in the microbial community could trigger the disease, in which the body kills cells that produce insulin.

Microbial disturbances could be at the root of other auto-immune disorders too.

Good microbes keep us slim

Microbes help our body by digesting and fermenting foods and by producing chemicals that shape our metabolic rates. Several microbes are linked to obesity in animals and humans. Animal and human viruses, bacteria, parasites and scrapie agents, increase adiposity (severely over weight) in several animal models. Infections can be exacerbated by impaired immune function of adipose tissue in obesity.

Good microbes detoxify and should even defend stress

Just as humans breath in oxygen and release carbon dioxide, microbes take in toxins and spare us their dangerous effects. A recent study shows that folks feeling intense stress have abundantly less microorganism communities within the gut. There can be a connection between microbes and stress responses. Some microbes (parasites, virus) may remain quiescent until activated sporadically by stress.

Microbes keep babies healthy

Recent studies have shown that babies born via C section delivery have different microbiomes than those born vaginally. Babies born vaginally are colonized with microbes of their mother, especially substances that aid in the digestion of milk. According to Science News, babies born via C-section are more likely to develop allergies and asthma than children born vaginally.

Step 4 to cancer free: kill the parasites first

Liver, colorectal and lymphoid tumors may be associated with parasites. Before my mother died of liver cancer, she took out a big parasite from her anus. Find anti-parasitic meds and natural ways to purge worms/parasites. Aloe vera, taken in any kind, is especially helpful in eliminating worms.

The following herbs help expel worms: cascara sagrada, wormwood seed, cloves, Echinacea, goldenseal, burdock, and black walnut. Do not use wormwood during pregnancy. Grapefruit seed extract helps destroy parasites.

Take black walnut extract and chaparral tea or tablets. Eat pumpkin seeds and figs. Also, drink the fig juice. Take diatomite capsules for three weeks, to get rid of your worms. (Do not imagine you do not have some; everyone generally does.) The worms eat this, and it causes them to disintegrate.

How

- Drink one cup of suffrutex with ginger (or sarsaparilla) tea 3 times daily between meals.
- Chinchona bark tea (1/2 teaspoon in 1 cup boiling water for 10 minutes) is bitter but effective.
- Elecampane contains 2 anti-amoebic compounds. Add 1 teaspoon to 1 cup boiling water, simmer 20 minutes, and drink 1-3 cups per day.
- Folk healers in India give turmeric and ginger for getting rid of worms, especially nematodes. It has 4 antiparasitic compounds.

Diet

Eat figs and pumpkin seeds. This can be combined with black walnuts. Pumpkin seeds and extracts immobilize and aid in the expulsion of intestinal worms. Because of its high tannin content, the kernel and green hull of black walnuts have been used to expel various worms by Asians and American Indians. External applications kill ringworm. Chinese use it to kill tapeworms.

Eat garlic, onions, cabbage, and carrots. They contain natural sulfur, which helps expel worms. As you may expect, worms do not like garlic.

Garlic is used for pinworms, roundworms, giardia (an amoeba), and other parasitic infections.

- Juice 3 cloves with 4-6 oz. carrot juice and take every 2 hours. Make sure you are obtaining enough water. Drink only pure water (distilled).
- To eliminate pinworms, eat 1-2 bitter melons each day for 7-10 days.

- To eliminate tapeworms, fast 3 days on raw pineapple. (The bromelain in it destroys the worms.)
- Cut up 2 raw onions and soak them twelve hours in one-pint water; straining whereas squeeze out the juice.
- Drink a cup of this three times daily. Along with this, use garlic enemas.
- Mix tansy, bitterroot, and wormwood; and put in capsules. Take two capsules, 4 times a day.
- For children, make senna tea, strain it, and add enough raisins to soak up the tea.

Pomegranate is used to expel roundworms and tapeworms. Grated raw apples, sprinkled with anise seed in a salad, is said to expel worms. In a study from July 2019 Frontiers in Microbiology, researchers found that the average apple contains 100 million bacteria on the inside.

Yarrow is a tonic to the bowels after worms have been expelled. Mexicans use cayenne to eliminate worms.

Fresh horseradish is effective against some worms, dropsy and digestive disorders. Tansy tea has been used by herbalists to expel worms. Eat thyme and oregano as they inhibit the parasites and aid in expelling them.

Other vermifuges include: bilberry, tarragon, European pennyroyal oil kills germs and keep insects away, quassia wood and bark, tamarind leaves, mugwort, and carline thistle.

Hormone therapy in prostate cancer tied to dementia and alzheimer's

Medications affect gut microbiome. A new study has found that many common meds (PPIs, metformin, antibiotics, laxatives) can predispose people to infections affecting the gut microbiome, increase risk for developing obesity and antimicrobial resistance (UEG Week 2019, University of Medical Center Groningen and Maastricht University Medical Center). Bad microbes in the gut can influence the brain and lead to dementia/ Alzheimers. As the immune system is affected by medications and gut microbes, the ability of the brain to detox and be free from microbes is influenced by the presence of medications and healthy gut microbes.

GI microbiome is involved in multiple-related processes such as modulation of circulating hormone levels. Stimulation of antitumor immune responses and induction of treatment-related toxicities, including immunotherapy-induced colitis and radiation-induced bowel toxicity and/or morbidities including development of metabolic syndrome.

Elderly patients with dementia or Alzheimer's disease may exhibit increased symptoms of confusion or agitation while taking Tramadol. Other meds that may contribute to dementia include: amitriptyline, paroxetine, and bupropion (most commonly taken for depression) oxybutynin and tolterodine (taken for an overactive bladder) diphenhydramine (a common antihistamine, as found in Benadryl)

Ginger and cinnamon kills parasites

Ginger may have cancer-battling characteristics. The study, published in Cancer Prevention Research, is an early advance toward seeing if mixes discovered in ginger root might prevent colon cancer.

Ginger, by supporting the digestive system, can help to kill parasites in the stomach before they pass on to the intestine. Once parasites have invaded the intestine, anti-parasitic herbs are needed, along with a careful diet, to rid the body of parasites.

Ginger and cinnamon caused reduction of **fecal cyst** and trophozoites counts. Cinnamon extracts in a study especially in a dose of 20 mg/kg/day were more effective than ginger not only in decreasing fecal cyst count but also in improving the histopathological and electron microscopic changes of intestinal mucosa.

Researchers found that the ginger concentrate has anticancer properties through p53 pathway to instigate apoptosis. My grandmother's back rub oil contains ginger, garlic, salt and different fixings. She utilizes it to normally rub her legs and different pieces of her body. She died at age 94 without any drugs as she created many homemade oils and herbs. She chews garlic and ginger regularly.

The root or underground stem (rhizome) of the ginger plant can be expended new, powdered, dried as a zest, in oil structure, or as juice. Ginger is a piece of the Zingiberaceae family, close by cardamom and turmeric.

It is accessible crisp and dried, as ginger concentrate and ginger oil, and in tinctures, cases, and capsules.

Conceivable medical advantages incorporate diminishing sickness, torment, and inflammation. Ginger can be utilized to make tea, cleaved or squashed in curries and flavourful dishes, and dried or crystallized in desserts.

Advantages

Root or powdered ginger adds flavor to numerous dishes, and it can profit wellbeing as well. Devouring products of the soil of different sorts has for some time been related with a decreased danger of numerous way of life related wellbeing conditions.

Logical examination demonstrates that ginger contains hundreds of compounds and metabolites, some of which may add to wellbeing and recuperation. Of these, the gingerols and shogaols have been most widely looked into.

Absorption of ginger

The phenolic mixes in ginger are known to help assuage gastrointestinal (GI) aggravation, animate spit and bile creation, and smother gastric withdrawals as nourishment and liquids travel through the GI tract.

Ginger affects the chemicals trypsin and pancreatic lipase, and to build motility through the stomach related tract. This proposes ginger could help prevent colon cancer and constipation.

Sickness

- Biting crude ginger or drinking ginger tea is a typical home solution for queasiness during cancer treatment.
- Taking ginger for movement affliction appears to lessen sentiments of sickness, however it doesn't seem to avert regurgitating.
- Ginger is protected to use during pregnancy, to ease sickness. It is accessible as ginger capsules or confections.

Cold and influenza alleviation

Chewing ginger can stop light coughing and early cold symptoms. During chilly climate, drinking ginger tea is a great approach to keep warm. It is diaphoretic, which implies that it advances perspiring, attempting to warm the body from inside.

To make ginger tea at home, cut 20 to 40 grams (g) of new ginger and soak it in some high temp water with a cut of lemon or a drop of honey to enhance and provide vitamin C and antibacterial properties. This makes a calming regular solution for a cold or flu.

Agony decrease

- An examination including 74 volunteers did at the College of Georgia found that day by day ginger supplementation decreased exercise-actuated muscle torment by 25 percent.
- Ginger has additionally been found to reduce the manifestations of dysmenorrhea, the extreme torment that a few women experience during a menstrual cycle.
- **Aggravation**
- Ginger has been utilized for a considerable length of time to lessen aggravation and treat incendiary conditions.
- An investigation distributed in Cancer Counteractive action Research journal detailed that ginger supplements, which are accessible to purchase on the web, decreased the hazard of colorectal cancer developing in the entrail of 20 volunteers.
- Ginger has likewise been found to be "modestly useful and sensibly protected" for treating aggravation related with osteoarthritis.

Cardiovascular wellbeing

Other conceivable uses include reducing cholesterol, bringing down the danger of blood coagulating, and keeping up solid glucose levels. More research is required, yet whenever demonstrated, ginger could turn out to be a piece of a treatment for heart disease and diabetes.

In our 50s, it is best to have fresh ginger tea for healthy circulatory system and to kill infections. In 100 grams (g) / 79 calories of crisp ginger root, here are its nutrients:

- 17.86 g of carbohydrate
- 3.6 g of dietary fiber
- 3.57 g of protein
- 0 g of sugar
- 14 mg of sodium
- 1.15 g of iron
- 7.7 mg of vitamin C
- 33 mg of potassium ; Older adults should also try to get 4,700 milligrams of potassium each day.
- Other nutrients found in ginger are:
- vitamin B6
- magnesium
- phosphorus
- zinc ; Zinc helps control infections by gently tapping the brakes on the immune response in a way that prevents out-of-control inflammation that can be damaging and even deadly.
- folate ; A megaloblastic type of anemia usually implies a deficiency of vitamin B12 or folic (pteroylglutamic) acid.
- riboflavin
- niacin

Balance your stress level for stress will show in your skin.

Key References

- Ding M, Leach M, Bradley H. The effectiveness and safety of ginger for pregnancy-induced nausea and vomiting: a systematic review. *Women and Birth*. 2013;26(1):e26-e30.
- Ginger. Natural Medicines Web site. Accessed at naturalmedicines. therapeuticresearch.com on April 15, 2015. [Database subscription].

- Ginger root. In: Blumenthal M, Goldberg A, Brinckmann J, eds. *Herbal Medicine: Expanded Commission E Monographs.* Newton, MA: Integrative Medicine Communications; 2000:153-159.
- Heitmann K, Nordeng H, Holst L. Safety of ginger use in pregnancy: results from a large population-based cohort study. *European Journal of Clinical Pharmacology.* 2013;69(2):269-277.
- Low Dog T. Ginger. In: Coates PM, Betz JM, Blackman MR, et al., eds. *Encyclopedia of Dietary Supplements.* 2nd ed. New York, NY: Informa Healthcare; 2010:325-331.
- Matthews A, Haas DM, O'Mathúna DP, et al. Interventions for nausea and vomiting in early pregnancy. Cochrane Database of Systematic Reviews. 2014;(3):CD007575. Accessed at http://www.thecochranelibrary.com on April 16, 2015.
- Pillai AK, Sharma KK, Gupta YK, et al. Anti-emetic effect of ginger powder versus placebo as an add-on therapy in children and young adults receiving high emetogenic chemotherapy. *Pediatric Blood & Cancer.* 2011;56(2):234-238.
- Ryan JL, Heckler CE, Roscoe JA, et al. Ginger *(Zingiber officinale)* reduces acute chemotherapy-induced nausea: a URCC CCOP study of 576 patients. *Supportive Care in Cancer.* 2012;20(7):1479-1489.

Parasitic worms and inflammatory diseases

The discussion on whether infection accelerates or prevents autoimmunity remains an issue. Recently the proposal that some unknown microbe can be at the birthplace of some chronic inflammatory diseases has been countered by collecting proof that decreasing infection rates may have a significant task to carry out in the rising prevalence of autoimmune disorders.

Note: Parasitic worm, Schistosomiasis, also known as bilharzia or snail fever, affects an estimated 207 million people, most of whom live in developing nations in tropical areas. About 20 million of those people with the disease become seriously disabled due to severe anemia, diarrhea, internal bleeding and/or organ damage. In addition, another 280,000 die of the disease each year.

Worm parasites have co-evolved with the mammalian immune

system for a large number of years and during this time, they have grown amazingly effective techniques to modulate and evade host guards thus keep up their developmental fitness. It is therefore sensible to presume that the human immune system has been molded by its relationship with parasitic worms and this might be an essential necessity for keeping up our immunological wellbeing.

WHY OUR BODIES ARE
TUNED TO FIGHT CANCER

Before we reach the age of 40 or even 50, our mitochondria and all our cells are working together to get rid of invading pathogens and weakening of our membranes. With air pollution, our lungs cannot provide the needed oxygen to all our cells. With the lack of CQ10 in our cells, there is less energy to put up a fight with the weakening of our cells.

With lack of sleep, our brain cannot detox our bodies. With the presence of sugar in the blood and amino acid alanine, cancer cells can grow slowly over time, around 30 years. Alcohol, nicotine and other endocrine disrupting substances in our lifestyle contribute to our fast aging. Our liver are overloaded with medications, parasites and other pathogens.

Many of those who lived past 100, have the following in their diet, plant foods such as yams or sweet potatoes, tofu, greens and fresh fish. They don't eat leftovers, only fresh foods. No reheating is needed, creating toxic nitrites. They are not living under stress but instead, they are surrounded by nature. In some European countries, there is a 3-day workweek once an adult reaches the age of 45.

Note: Persistent pathogens: Unlike acute infections, which are cleared after mobilization of the immune system, persistent infections do not result in sterilizing immunity. Virologists that study herpes viruses think that all herpes viruses become latent. By contrast, hepatitis C virus and HIV are considered chronic persistent viruses (doi: 10.1038/nri2318).

Our bodies can identify and fight any invading pathogens and substances and our liver can regenerate when we are young. As we age, our cells are weaker to fight these pathogens and toxins with our membranes weak and have less energy. We get energy from sleep, sunshine, clean air and water and other nutrients from plant foods.

Detox your lungs from air pollution and metal toxins and for early lung cancer

Liposomal Vitamin C

When my father died of lung cancer in 2002, I have been researching about how to get rid of the toxins in our lungs. Liposomal Vitamin C and amino acid Lysine were listed to help stop early stage lung cancer.

Turmeric and green tea tell our body master antioxidant Glutathione to work harder. Enzymes of guava, pineapple, papaya and mango help in breaking down more toxins.

Broccoli sprouts, the more potent greens, help in detoxing air pollution (especially indoor air from our own house and cars). While our genes predispose us to cancers (affect 15% in growth, stress can double cancer growth, sugar is the food of cancer cells and a strong immune system is our ultimate weapon), our lymphatic system must be taken cared for.

If I have early stage lung cancer, I will soak my body in sea water, relaxing on the beach, taking in fresh air. I would nap more in the afternoon, relax when tired, sleep well and get massaged with essential oils of eucalyptus, frankincense, sage, thyme and melaleuca.

Know that sugar is food for cancer cells. A powerful chicken soup that my mom makes contains Malunggay or Moringa (powerful healing greens) and some companies are selling them in powder, protein bars and many forms.

Anti-aging and Parkinson/Alzheimer's prevention: apple cider and enzymes

Boosting Your Enzymes Levels Naturally
There are four different ways to naturally increase your enzyme levels:

- Increase your intake of raw, living foods
- Eat fewer calories

- Chew your food thoroughly
- Avoid chewing gum. Chew gum after eating not on empty stomach. When chewing gum, acid is secreted into the stomach, important when food is present but not on an empty stomach. This leads to a build up of unnecessary acid in the stomach.

The best approach to get enzymes into your body is by consuming 70% at least on your raw foods. For many of you, you'll have to work toward this goal gradually. While all raw foods contain enzymes, the powerful-enzyme rich foods are those that are sprouted. Sprouting increases the enzyme content in these foods tremendously.

Besides sprouts, other enzyme-rich foods include:

- Papaya, pineapple, mango, kiwi, and grapes
- Avocado
- Raw honey (the enzymes originate from the honey bee's spit)
- Bee pollen
- Additional virgin olive oil and coconut oil
- Raw dairy

The best approach to knock up your metabolic enzymes is to provide your body with the raw materials and energy it needs to make them.

Methionine-restricted diet (high in hydrogen sulfide, foul smelling gas promotes growth in our cells) do NOT contain:

- Brazil Nuts
- Lean Beef & Lamb (Roast Beef)
- Cheese (Parmesan)
- Turkey & Chicken (Chicken Breast, cooked)
- Pork (Sirloin, cooked)

Hydrogen sulfide gives rotten eggs their characteristic odor, is also made in our cells where it functions in many beneficial ways. One of these is to promote the growth of **new blood vessels from endothelial cells**—a process known as angiogenesis.

Lack of oxygen, or hypoxia, is the best-described trigger of angiogenesis. Hypoxia happens in tissues when a vessel is blocked, or upon intense exercise when oxygen delivery is constrained. Methionine restriction activated angiogenesis regardless of normal oxygen delivery, recommending involvement of a pathway detecting amino acid deprivation as opposed to hypoxia.

Large amounts of methionine can be found in eggs, meat, and fish; sesame seeds and some other plant seeds; and oat grains.

Protozoan parasites in humans

Three protozoan parasites of humans, Entamoeba histolytica, Giardia intestinalis, and Trichomonas vaginalis, share various biological and biochemical characteristics, including anaerobic carbohydrate metabolism and the lack of typical mitochondria.

As parasites, these organisms have a reduced ability for the de novo (anew) synthesis of essential building blocks of DNA and proteins, including nucleic acid precursors and amino acids. As a consequence, certain metabolic pathways either are missing in these organisms.

Proper hygiene and washing of foods to prevent parasites entry

T. gondii can infect virtually all warm-blooded animals, but only cats (both wild and domestic) serve as the definitive host and can excrete up to 800 million infective oocysts in their feces (64). A recent survey of cats at spay/neuter clinics in Ohio revealed that 48% of all cats were infected with T. gondii, with a higher incidence in outdoor cats.

These oocysts can survive for long periods in the environment and may be spread by the wind or by a variety of insects and earthworms and contaminate foods ingested by humans and other animals.

Humans are the only known host for this roundworm. Eggs passed out with feces may be ingested by the same or another person who drinks contaminated water, eats with dirty hands, or eats uncooked vegetables that have been fertilized with contaminated human waste. Liver flukes have a complex life cycle involving two intermediate hosts, snails and fish.

Washing of foods: I use salt in water and diluted vinegar to wash veggies.

Raw fish can contain Anisakis and some other less common parasites and, if it is to be eaten raw, should first be frozen to kill the parasites. There is a potential risk that raw shellfish will contain protozoan parasites, such as Cryptosporidium. Elderly and immunocompromised persons should avoid or be very cautious about consuming raw meat, fish, or shellfish.

Pyruvate supply is critical to parasite growth

Toxoplasma gondii is a widespread intracellular pathogen infecting humans and a variety of animals. Previous studies have shown that Toxoplasma uses glucose and glutamine as the main carbon sources to support asexual reproduction, but neither nutrient is essential. Such metabolic flexibility may allow it to survive within diverse host cell types.

Catabolism of all indicated carbon sources converges at pyruvate, and maintaining a constant pyruvate supply is critical to parasite growth. The top food sources of beta-alanine are meat, poultry and fish. It is a part of larger compounds — mainly carnosine and anserine — but breaks free when they are digested. Vegetarians and vegans have about 50% less carnosine in their muscles compared to omnivores.

Pyruvate rich foods

Pyruvate forms in the body when carbohydrates and protein convert into energy. Several foods, including red apples, cheese, dark beer, and red wine, contain small amounts of pyruvate. Pyruvate provides energy to the body and is also an antioxidant. It enhances weight loss efforts and may improve exercise endurance.

Parasites and microbes need triglycerides or cholesterol to thrive

Parasites thrive on cholesterol. During infection huge changes in lipid digestion and lipoprotein synthesis happen. Triglyceride and VLDL cholesterol levels increase, while reduced HDL cholesterol (HDL-C) and LDL cholesterol (LDL-C) levels are observed. Cholesterol starvation initiates encystations. This indicates that cholesterol has a role in pathogenesis as it helps the parasite to remain in trophozoite stage. (Lipids Health Dis. 2005; 4: 10. Published online 2005 May 9. doi: 10.1186/1476-511X-4-10)

HDLs are rising as an applicable player during parasitic diseases and a particular segment of HDL, apoL-1, presents inborn invulnerability against trypanosome by favoring lysosomal swelling which kills the parasite.

Low levels of vitamin D in cancer and parasites-infection related health issue

Early signs of disease shows deficiency in vitamin D. Parasites, infections, inflammation, auto-immune disease and cancer shows low levels of vitamin D. Accumulating evidence singles out several candidates, including sunlight-UV exposure or vitamin D deficiency, viral infections, hygiene, and cigarette smoking. Vitamin D deficiency has been related with various immune system ailments.

Note: Vitamin D can modulate the innate and adaptive immune responses. Deficiency in vitamin D is associated with increased autoimmunity as well as an increased susceptibility to infection. (J Investig Med. 2011 Aug; 59(6): 881–886. doi: 10.231/JIM.0b013e31821b8755)

Foods to avoid and to prevent diabetes

Eat in moderation, consume more whole foods and fiber-rich foods and avoid processed foods to prevent diabetes and to lower triglycerides.

- Sugar-sweetened beverages/sodas
- White bread, pasta and rice
- Fruit-Flavored Yogurt
- Sweetened breakfast cereals
- Flavored coffee drinks
- Honey, agave nectar and maple syrup
- Dried fruit
- Burnt BBQ meat
- Trans fats
- Wafers, treats, cakes, solidified pies, and other baked goods.
- Snack foods (such as microwave popcorn)
- Frozen pizza
- Fast-food
- Vegetable shortenings and some stick margarines
- Coffee creamer

- Refrigerated batter items, (for example, scones and cinnamon rolls)
- Processed foods rich in nitrites and also left over foods

Anti-parasites diet

Up to nearly 10% of Americans may be infected with brain parasites found in undercooked meat. One example is the brain-invasive pork tapeworm, which is the most common cause of adult-onset epilepsy. Allergenic fish worms found in almost 66% of retail fish tested can trigger allergic reaction in delicate/sensitive people.

There have been migratory skin worms found in half-cooked fish (like in sushi). Cheese may contain parasites and slimy parasites and organ meats may contain different worms.

Cheese: Asiago, bel paese, bleu/blue, brick, brie, camembert, emmental, gorgonzola, gruyere, muenster, port de salut, roquefort, stilton, swiss, pork.

Nearly 95% of tested retail U.S. meat (including burgers) has been observed to be parasite plagued.

The meat business has reacted to this issue by encouraging arsenic to chickens and turkeys to reduce the parasite load. Arsenic might be connected to increased risk of cancer. Adding bacteria-eating viruses to meat would not help one to keep away the brain parasite, toxoplasma, the second leading reason for food-borne sickness related death in the US.

Avoid cheese, under-cooked meat, salads and produce not properly washed with vinegar or salt water, over ripe fruits. Eat limes and berries, pineapple and papaya, sweet potatoes or yams, pine nuts, and eat less on fermented foods (except fiber-rich).

Consume less fat and sugar filled and processed foods but eat more fiber-rich foods, freshly cooked and well cooked.

Combine meat with veggies. Drisk less alcohol drinks. Add cabbage, ginger, tomatoes and lemon when cooking fish or meat to kill the parasites. Boil milk if you wanted to drink 2% milk. Drink less milk, although goat milk is preferred.

Add garlic, onions and sulfur rich foods in your meals daily. Eat well washed raw carrots and garlic. Have a banana at night (not over ripe). Avoid caffeine and chocolate until you have completed your anti-parasitic meds.

Lowering your fat intake from keto diet, lowers the supply of cholesterol for parasites to thrive. Use all kinds of coconut from oil to milk. Do not consume 3-day old rice or left over foods. Wear gloves when washing fish. Promote good hygiene.

Freeze fish for portion you cannot eat within 2 days. Do not eat wilted veggies or moldy and rotten. Search this site for food, anti-inflammation, sulfur rich foods, diet, toxins.

Gut bacteria's connections to human health and disease

Learning the components by which gut microbes influence the strength of their hosts opens the door to the development of better, increasingly customized diagnostic techniques and treatments.

Metagenomics refers to the study of genetic material recouped directly from natural examples — for this situation, human fecal examples — instead of from life forms cultured in a lab. A meta-investigation is a statistical method for combining information from different studies.

The meta-analysis performed by Armour, Sharpton and their colleagues included metagenomic information from almost 2,000 feces tests gathered for studies including colorectal cancer, Crohn's disease, liver cirrhosis, obesity, rheumatoid arthritis, type 2 diabetes and ulcerative colitis.

The gut microbiota includes in excess of 10 trillion microbial cells from around 1,000 distinctive bacterial species. The microbial ecosystem remains in balance through cell-to-cell signaling and the release of antimicrobial peptides that hold in line certain bacterial clades.

Gut microorganisms interact with their human host too, sometimes in ways that promote health, different occasions in manners that add to disease development. Dysbiosis, or imbalance, in the microbiome is generally connected with negative impacts to the host's wellbeing.

Gut microbiome useful beta-scattering is diverse among healthy and diseased populaces and saw an expansion in functional beta-scattering in patients with colorectal cancer, Crohn's disease and liver cirrhosis. People with obesity showed decreased Beta dispersion in relative to their controls.

Beta dispersion is a phenomenon associated with the ability of a biological cell membrane to filter out low frequency currents and allow high frequency currents to pass through.

Root causes of chronic illness

During the last 20 years, your body is exposed to inflammation such as over consumption of sugar, stress and trauma, gut bacteria/parasites/fungus/virus, lack of sleep and other chronic disease which can be prevented before it becomes Type 2 diabetes, depression, hypertension and even cancer.

1. As we age, we are 10,000 times more prone to attacks from parasites and cancer.
2. If we don't get our 8 hour night time sleep, we are slowly breaking down the barriers in our cell mucosa making it possible for unhealthy microbes to travel to other sites from liver to blood and then brain.
3. It takes cancer to overpower our cells at least 20 years. Know signs, detox your body starting with your liver and use whole foods such as apples with 100 million healthy bacteria to help fight invading pathogens. **Do avoid these environmental toxins, feeding on weakened cells invaded by parasites, molds, fungus and virus.**
4. It's also important to focus on diet and encourage healthy lifestyle. Depression was associated with multiple inflammatory and even haemorrhagic gastro-intestinal complications, which may be due to side effects from medications used to treat depression, or even due to the greater occurrence of e-coli infections, both of which could be prevented.

What is the role of the gut microbiota in nutrition and health

Microbiome refers to the collective genomes of the microorganisms that are in a particular environment, and microbiota is simply the community of microorganisms. Roughly 100 trillion micro-organisms (the majority of them microscopic organisms, yet in addition infections, parasites, and protozoa) exist in the human gastrointestinal tract - the microbiome is currently best idea of as a virtual organ of the body.

The human genome comprises of about 23,000 qualities, while the microbiome encodes more than 3,000,000 qualities creating a large number of metabolites, which replace a significant number of the functions of the host, thus affecting the host's wellness, phenotype, and wellbeing.

We are entering a time where we can progressively alter health through food and measure the impacts through our microbes or metabolites. Eating plant polysaccharides (fruits, vegetables, whole grains, and legumes) as dietary fiber has been linked with multiple health benefits.

The gut–hormone connection: how gut organisms impact estrogen levels

To modulate estrogen levels, the gut microbiome secrets bioactive metabolites: short chain fatty acids, reactivated estrogen, amino acid metabolites and secondary bile acids. These tasks impact the danger of creating estrogen-related diseases (for example, endometriosis, polycystic ovary disorder, bosom disease, and prostate cancer).

With heavy bleeding in my 40s, I was told by my naturophatic doctor that hormonal balancing and liver cleansing herbs can work well. I took these herbs to cleanse my liver together with Vitamin C, B complex and magnesium/calcium (40:60 ratio).

Scientific research has shown that gut microorganisms manage numerous parts of human physiology, including intestinal penetrability, the ingestion of supplements from sustenance, and resistance. The estrobolome is the collection of microbes equipped for using estrogens. The estrobolome adjusts the enterohepatic course of estrogens and influences flowing and discharged estrogen levels.

Gut Dysbiosis Is Connected to Estrogen-Related Diseases

Estrogen assumes numerous crucial roles in the human body. It controls fat deposition and adipocyte differentiation, female reproductive function, cardiovascular health, bone turnover, and cell replication. Gut dysbiosis can possibly modify the estrobolome (gut microbiome affects estrogen), upset estrogen homeostasis, and weaken these procedures, promoting the improvement of chronic diseases.

Weight, Cardiovascular Disease, and Osteoporosis

In postmenopausal women, estrobolome interruption is related with an expanded risk of obesity, cardiovascular disease, and osteoporosis. Estrogens control glucose and lipid metabolism, adipocyte differentiation, bone development, and the inflammatory reaction in atherosclerosis. Research shows that the typical decreases in estrogen that happens at menopause hinder these estrogen-dependent procedures, triggering obesity, cardiovascular disease, and osteoporosis.

Foods to balance our estrogen levels include fruits and nuts (flaxseeds, small seed, pumpkin seeds).

Endometriosis

Endometriosis, an estrogen-driven condition described by the development of endometrial tissue outside the uterus, has been related with gut dysbiosis. The estrobolome of women with endometriosis may have bigger numbers of beta-glucuronidase-producing bacteria (E. coli), prompting increased levels of circling estrogen, which drives endometriosis. Research shows that bromelain (pineapple) can help counteract the effects of intestinal pathogens such as *E. coli* that cause diarrhea, and it may also reduce gastrointestinal tract inflammation.

Note: Escherichia coli, Bacteroides species, and Clostridium perfringens were the only species found to *produce beta-glucuronidase (Scand J Gastroenterol. 1988 Jan;23(1):83-90.)*

PCOS

Polycystic ovary syndrome (PCOS) may also be affected by estrobolome disruption. Women with PCOS have an excess of Androgens in connection to estrogen, just as an adjusted gut microbiota. Analysts estimate that the changed gut microbiota in PCOS women may promote increased androgen biosynthesis and decreased estrogen levels through lowered beta-glucuronidase activity.

Probiotics Can Restore a Healthy Estrogen Balance

Research demonstrates that it might be possible to modulate the estrobolome and turn around estrogen-related pathologies through probiotic supplementation.

- Supplementation with a broad range of Lactobacillus probiotic has been found to standardize the estrous cycle and decrease testosterone biosynthesis in animal model of PCOS.
- In an animal model of endometriosis, Lactobacillus gasseri prevented ectopic tissue development, which is an estrogen-driven procedure.
- In a menopausal mouse model of osteoporosis, Lactobacillus reuteri anticipated bone misfortune coming about because of low estrogen.
- Lactobacilli have anticarcinogenic effects in breast tissue, proposing that supplementation might be helpful for the prevention of breast cancer.
- While research on the connection between probiotic supplementation and the estrobolome is still in its earliest stages, this shouldn't prevent professionals from prescribing probiotics to their patients with estrogen-related conditions. Switching dysbiosis gives off an impression of being key for adjusting the estrobolome, and probiotic supplementation is a generally simple and cheap approach to achieve this.

How can I boost my immune system

A stronger immune system means that our bodies can easily get rid of toxins. Our lymphatic system that travels opposite our circulatory system cleans our blood. Lymphatic massage includes massaging the armpit, thighs, and exercise.

Genetics play a role and how we are conceived, birthed, and raised (environmental) shape how our cells can fight toxins (meds/drugs, alcohol, cigarettes, sugar, processed foods, lack of sleep, stress) as they enter our body.

If I have a bag of food for the immune system, it will include: happiness/nurture, sleep (our brain allows us to detox/cleanse our cells during sleep), massage, exercise, wholefoods (portion control avoiding consumption of sugar) and following herbs/oil - mucolytics aiding lysosomes in the destruction of toxins (authophagy): Astralagus, garlic/yellow colored foods, elecampane, coltsfoot, eucalyptus and tea tree, mullein, echinacea, rosemary, lavender, thyme, sage, bay and fenugreek seeds.

Triggering the immune system for cancer patients

One way in which a fasting diet may help cancer patients is by triggering the immune system. The immune system is designed to target and destroy pathogens in the body, like viruses. However, it seems to be less able to find, target, and kill the body's own abnormal cells, like cancer cells. A lot of new cancer treatments are being developed to stimulate the immune system to do this, but new research is finding that a simple fasting diet could also do it.

More autoimmune diseases in women than men

An autoimmune disease is a condition emerging from an abnormal immune response to a normal body part. There are at least 80 types of autoimmune diseases.Nearly any body part can be involved.

Commons symptoms include poor quality fever and feeling tired. Often symptoms come and go. Researchers believe that gene mutations, the environment and even the human microbiome are involved in autoimmune diseases, citing such environmental stimuli as smoking, obesity, sun exposure and infection with the Epstein-Barr virus.

These diseases regularly keep running in families and, while uncommon,some people can experience the effects of more than one at the same time known as poly-autoimmunity. Mismatch between environment and genes appears to be an autoimmune disease.

Women typically mount a more vigorous immune response than men to diseases and immunizations, creating more elevated amounts of antibodies.Scientists believe that sex hormones also may play a role, because many autoimmune disorders happen in women not long after puberty.

Gut bacteria drives autoimmune disease

A recent study in mice uncovers that persistent social stress changes gut microbiota, or microorganisms, in manners that can trigger certain immune reactions.

Autoimmune conditions are created when the immune system assaults the body's own tissues, organs, and cells. It reacts to them just as they were disease causing bacteria and viruses.

The National Institute of Allergy and Infectious Diseases recommend that there are in any event 80 autoimmune disease, including lupus, rheumatoid joint inflammation, and type 1 diabetes.

Studies have recognized s**tress as a risk factor for autoimmune diseases.**

Specialists at Bar Ilan University in Israel have now discovered that gut bacteria in mice react to social stress by increasing the quantity of effector T helper cells, immune cells that assume a job in autoimmunity.

Manifestations change in autoimmune diseases

The reasons for many diseases to happen much more in women than in men are not clear. Beside acquired dangers, researchers presume that the odds of building up an autoimmune disease emerge for the most part from complex interactions among genes and environment. A disease frequently begins with vision issues and develops to weakness and difficulties with balance and coordination (leg and knee pain).

In contrast, in the uncommon and disabling disease scleroderma, autoimmunity prompts fibrosis, which is the overproduction of collagen and different proteins that structure connective tissue. Scleroderma can influence different parts of the body, including inner organs, skin, and veins. The various kinds of disease shift by the extent to which fibrosis is limited or systematic (affecting various organs and tissues).

Stress adjusts gut bacteria in mice

Researchers found that the social pressure/stressed group had more Bilophila and Dehalobacterium than the controls. Researchers have also discovered more elevated amounts of these gut bacteria in individuals with

Multiple Sclerosis. Researchers discovered that there is a chain of occasions whereby

1. stress introduction
2. changes to gut bacteria
3. and changes to immune cells
4. lead to a higher risk of an autoimmune attack

A healthy diet vs. autoimmune disease

Our bodies have the ability to make antibodies to shield us from bad microbes like bacteria, parasites and viruses. Certain triggers can start the generation of antibodies against our own solid tissues. A malfunctioning immune system can assault and harm practically any piece of the body.

Autoimmune disease consists of more than 80 health conditions that resulted in an over-active immune system. Upwards of 23 million individuals – 78% of whom are women in the US have autoimmune disease.

One case of the potential connection between the gut microbiome and immune system ailment can be found in Sort 1 diabetes (T1D), a malady where the body assaults and crushes insulin-creating cells in the pancreas.

So what would we be able to eat to help counteract immune system issues?

Whole foods and not processed foods are best choices for our immune system. Important foods include ginger, garlic, onions, carrots, kiwi, pineapple, root crops and colorful whole foods. Most seniors who are bed ridden have lots of canned and frozen foods in their kitchen. An eating routine brimming with processed foods stacked with refined sugar/flour with added substances, synthetic compounds, unsafe fats, and an absence of fiber appear to adversely influence well being and an individual's gut microbiome.

Mind controlling parasites

Envision a parasite that makes an animal change its propensities, monitor the parasite's offspring or even end it all. While mind-control may sound like something out of a sci-fi film, the marvel is genuine — and has brought forth another field, neuro-parasitology.

One technique is to influence how an insect navigates. The spores of one parasitic fungus, for instance, attack an insect's body, where the fungus develops and devours the insect's organs while leaving the organs intact. The parasite at that point discharges chemicals that reason the subterranean insect to climb a tree and grasp a leaf with its mouth parts.

After emerging from the insect's body, the organism discharges spore-filled containers that detonate throughout their fall, spreading the irresistible spores over the ground beneath. By forcing the insect to climb a tree, the fungus increase the dispersal of the falling spores and the possibility of infecting another ant.

A parasitic hair worm makes infected crickets search out water — where they suffocate. The cricket's suicide enables the worms to enter a sea-going environment for reproduction.

In another sort of collaboration, called "guardian control," the parasite forces the infected insect to monitor its young. One such parasite is a wasp, which infuses its eggs into a caterpillar by stinging it. Inside the live caterpillar, its eggs bring forth into hatchlings, which feed on the caterpillar's blood. In the end, upwards of 80 hatchlings rise up out of the caterpillar's body before framing covers to finish their development into grown-up wasps.

Exercise may improve health by increasing gut bacterial diversity

Bacteria frequently synonymous with infection and disease, may have an unjustifiable reputation. Research demonstrates there are the same number of, if not increasingly, bacterial cells in our bodies as human cells, which means they assume a significant job in our physiology.

A study in Experimental Psychology has recommended that the effectiveness with which we transport oxygen to our tissues (cardiorespiratory fitness) is a predictor of gut microbiota decent variety than either muscle to fat percentage or general physical activity.

Cardiorespiratory fitness (CRF) refers to the ability of the circulatory and respiratory systems to supply oxygen to skeletal muscles during sustained physical activity.

Exercise induces changes in skeletal muscle to purge the blood from toxins. 20 minutes of exercise can act as anti-inflammatory. Aerobic exercise and HITT training make telomeres in the brain to grow longer. Belly fat can be reduced with exercise, sage tea, protein-rich and vitamin C-rich foods. Waste products of exercise protect neurons from trauma damage. Leg exercise is critical to brain and nervous system health.

It was understood that higher cardiorespiratory fitness would in general correspond with more noteworthy gut microbiota assorted variety, yet it was vague whether this relationship was attributable from muscle to fat percentage or physical exercises of daily-living.

Gut bacteria interferes with metabolism of parkinson's medication

The majority who head to the kitchen to prepare a serving of mixed salad dressing, pop popcorn, age vegetables, or caramelize onions, did not think about the crucial chemical reactions behind these mixtures.

More critical are the responses that occur after the plates are clean. At the point when a slice of sourdough goes through the digestive system, the trillions of microbes that live in our gut help the body break down that bread to retain the nutrients. Since the human body can't process certain substances—terrifically significant fiber, for instance microbes venture up to perform science no human can.

Concentrating on levodopa (L-dopa), the essential treatment for Parkinson's disease, they distinguished which bacteria out of the trillions of species is in charge of degrading the medication and how to stop this microbial interference.

Parkinson's disease attacks **nerve cells in the brain** that produce dopamine, without which the body can endure tremors, muscle rigidity, and issues with balance and coordination. L-dopa conveys dopamine to the brain to relieve symptoms. Yet, just around **1 to 5%** of the medication really reaches the brain.

Researchers realized that the body's enzymes (instruments that perform essential science) can separate L-dopa in the gut, keeping the medication from arriving at the brain.

A food microbe frequently found in milk and pickles (Lactobacillus brevis), can acknowledge both tyrosine and L-dopa.

After E. faecalis changes over the medication into dopamine, a second organism being changes over dopamine into another compound, meta-tyramine. Feeding dopamine to swarms of microbes to see which succeeded.

Dopamine-rich foods

- Dairy foods such as milk, cheese and yogurt
- Unprocessed meats such as beef, chicken and turkey
- Omega-3 rich fish such as salmon and mackerel
- Eggs
- Fruit and vegetables, in particular bananas
- Nuts such as almonds and walnuts
- Dark chocolate

Neurodegenerative disease links gastrointestinal tract – Parkinson's

The earliest evidence that the gut may be engaged with Parkinson's risen over 200 years back. In 1817, the English specialist James Parkinson revealed that a few patients with a condition he named "shaking palsy" experienced constipation.

From that point forward, doctors have noticed that constipation is one of the most well-known symptoms of Parkinson's, showing up in around a large portion of the people diagnosed have the condition and often preceding before the beginning of development related impairments.

THE GUT-Brain Highway

The vagus nerve, a bundle of fibers that starts in the brain stem and innervates major organs, including the gut, might be the essential course through which neurotic triggers of Parkinson's movement from the gastrointestinal tract to the brain. Recent epidemiological examinations of vagotomy patients whose vagus nerves were cut off demonstrate that they have a lower risk of developing Parkinson's.

Alpha-synuclein fibers, infused into the gastrointestinal tracts of rodents, can cross through the vagus into the brain.

Microbes themselves are another potential trigger for advancing the development of intestinal alpha-synuclein. Researchers have discovered that, in mice, bacterial proteins could trigger the total of the alpha-synuclein in the gut and the brain.

Clear your lungs from microorganisms

Steam therapy

Steam therapy, or steam inhalation, includes breathing in water vapor to open the airways and help the lungs channel bodily fluid. Individuals with lung conditions may see their side effects worsening in cold or dry air. This atmosphere can dry out the mucous films in the airways and confine blood stream.

Alternately, steam adds warmth and dampness to the air, which may improve breathing and help release bodily fluid inside the airways and lungs. Breathing in water vapor can give immediate relief and help individuals breathe easily.

A small study involving 16 males with chronic obstructive pulmonary disease (COPD), a lung condition that makes it harder to breathe, found that steam mask therapy led to significantly lower pulses and respiratory rates than non-steam mask therapy.

Controlled coughing

Controlled coughing can help send mucus through the airways. Coughing is the body's method for normally expelling toxins that it has caught in mucus. Fold the arms over the stomach, slowly inhale through the nose. Slowly breathe out while inclining forward, pushing the arms against the stomach, cough two or multiple times while breathing out, keeping the mouth marginally open. Slowly inhale through the nose. Rest and repeat as necessary.

Drain mucus from the lungs

Postural drainage involves lying in different positions to use gravity to remove mucus from the lungs. This training may improve breathing and help treat or prevent lung infections.

Postural drainage techniques differ depending on the position:

a. On your back lie down on the floor or a bed. Place pillows under the hips to ensure that the chest is lower than the hips. Slowly inhale through the nose and exhale through the mouth. Each breathe out should accept twice the length of breathe in, which is called 1:2 breathing. Continue for a few minutes.

b. On your side Lie on one side, resting the head on an arm or pillow. Place pillows under the hips. Practice the 1:2 breathing pattern. Continue for a few minutes. Repeat on the other side.

c. On your stomach Place a stack of pillows on the floor. Lie down with the stomach over the pillows. Remember to keep the hips above the chest. Fold the arms under the head for support. Practice the 1:2 breathing pattern. Continue for a few minutes. What happens after you quit smoking?

Exercise Regularly

Exercise can improve individuals' physical and psychological wellness, and it diminishes the danger of numerous well being conditions, including stroke and coronary illness. Exercise powers the muscles to work more earnestly, which expands the body's breathing rate. It additionally improves circulation, making the body progressively effective in removing the excess carbon dioxide that the body produces when working out. The body will start to adapt to meet the demands of regular exercise.

The muscles will learn to use oxygen more efficiently and produce less carbon dioxide. Although exercising may be more difficult for people with chronic lung conditions, these individuals can am regular exercise. People who have COPD, cystic fibrosis, or asthma should consult a healthcare professional before starting a new exercise regimen.

Green Tea

Green tea contains many antioxidants that may help lessen inflammation in the lungs. These compounds may even shield lung tissue from the destructive impacts of smoke inhalation, fungal spores and parasites. Green tea's polyphenol shielded mice from tumors of the liver, *lungs*, skin. *Green tea* strengthens the immune system to fight viruses, *fungi* and bacteria. Green tea catechins have also been shown to be effective against a number of viruses, parasites, fungi, and even prions. Prions characterize several fatal and transmissible neurodegenerative diseases in humans and many other animals.

Sage tea

When rodents were given sage *tea* instead of water for two weeks, their liver antioxidant activity increased by 10–24%.That includes certain *parasites*, bacteria, and *fungi*. The *parasite* can also infect your *lungs*, brain, and spinal cord. Sage, garlic, thyme, cinnamon, mustard and oregano have anti-microbial properties.

Inflammatory foods (raw meat, soy oil, processed foods, burned meat, white sugar, moldy foods, left overs, milk, reheated left overs, nitrites)

Eating cherries can help fight inflammation. Inflammation of the airways can make breathing difficult and cause the chest to feel heavy and congested. Eating anti-inflammatory foods can reduce inflammation to relieve these symptoms. Foods that help fight inflammation include: turmeric, leafy greens, cherries, blueberries, olives,walnuts,beans, lentils, ginger onions, garlic or sulfur-rich foods.

Note: Under certain conditions in the human body, *nitrite* can damage cells and also morph into molecules that cause cancer. Nitrate is harmless, but it can be converted to nitrites, and then to nitrosamines. Enzymes present in bacteria convert nitrate to nitrite. This happens especially when spinach is heated, stored and then later reheated. And is true for other whole foods.

Inorganic dietary nitrate, found abundantly in green leafy and some root vegetables, elicits several beneficial physiological effects, including a reduction in blood pressure and improvements in blood flow through nitrate–nitrite–nitric oxide signaling (*Nutrition Reviews*, Volume 77, Issue 8, August 2019, Pages 584–599, https://doi.org/10.1093/nutrit/nuz025).

Beetroot or beet juice

Beets and beet juice are among the best food sources of nitrate. Beet juice might improve athletic performance because the body converts some of this nitrate to nitric oxide, which expands blood vessels. This blood vessel expansion increases blood flow and the delivery of oxygen and nutrients to exercising muscle. The expanded blood vessels also speed up the removal of waste products that cause muscle fatigue. Other nitrate rich foods include garlic, meat, dark chocolate, leafy greens, citrus fruits, pomegranate and nuts and seeds.

Chest percussion

Percussion is another successful method to remove excess mucus from the lungs. A healthcare professional or respiratory therapist will utilize a measured hand to rhythmically tap the chest divider to oust caught bodily fluid in the lungs. Joining chest percussion and postural waste can help clear the aviation routes of overabundance bodily fluid.

Mullein herb for breast and lung health

Mullein is indicated for dry, harsh, hacking coughs, and weak lungs. The flowers of this plant are soothing and coat the lungs, while the leaves are more astringent and expectorant, helping the lungs to expel unwanted particles that have been inhaled. Mullein is typically used for hoarseness, coughs, bronchitis, asthma and other respiratory conditions. Prepare tea by placing 1 teaspoon into 1 cup of hot water, or in combination with other lung loving herbs in the form of a tincture. Add ginger, lemon and garlic in the herbal tea.

Chronic obstructive pulmonary disease

COPD or what we call chronic obstructive pulmonary disease describes a lung conditions that cause extreme shortness of breath and block the airways in your lungs. It also refers to long-lasting bronchitis or emphysema, however can also include asthmatic bronchitis (bronchial asthma).

A scar tissue forms in the lungs, which don't permit in as much oxygen as you need. With emphysema, the walls of your lungs lose their elasticity — they can't constrict to allow you to exhale.

Signs and Symptoms

Ongoing cough, often with phlegm that may be hard to "bring up"

- Shortness of breath, especially during exercise.
- Production of increased mucus
- Difficulty exhaling
- Wheezing
- Frequent respiratory infections

Causes

Smoking is the primary cause of COPD. It can also be caused by exposure to pollutants or toxic chemicals or **toxins (fungus, microbes, parasites, mold, chemical fumes).** One rare form of COPD is inherited.

Preventive Care

- If you smoke, quit.
- If you have COPD, avoiding respiratory infections is very important. Your doctor will recommend that you receive an influenza vaccine (flu shot) each year and a pneumococcal vaccine to protect you from pneumonia.

Eating foods rich in folate, Vitamin C, antioxidants, magnesium and other minerals, and omega-3 fatty acids (including fruits, vegetables, and fish) may help lower your risk for COPD.

Nicotine and cocaine have same effects

Tobacco, cigar, cigar pipes contain nicotines with same effects as cocaine and alcohol. Nicotine and its connection with a systemic fungal infection. While a cigarette is a toxic cocktail of chemicals, none is so powerful as nicotine.

Nicotine mimics acetylcholine, the most prevalent neurotransmitter in the brain.

Acetylcholine aids basic muscle function, hand-eye coordination, and complex neurological responses and allows dopamine to turn the body to feel joy and pleasure.

Nicotine isn't controlled by the cerebrum, which means that the amount you consume is the amount that stimulates the acetylcholine receptors.

At the point when acetylcholine receptors are initiated, they discharge dopamine, which at that point makes the calming dopamine reaction most smokers experience when they have a cigarette.

Another neurotransmitter that is activated by nicotine is glutamate.

Involved in both long-term and short-term memory retention, the stimulation of glutamate while dopamine is being released creates a deeply entrenched memory of pleasure related to the consumption of nicotine.

This chemical reaction, repeated on numerous occasions every day, is the thing that makes such an intense addiction.

While the nicotine is tricking your mind into thinking it is acetylcholine, it is also doing something different.

Nicotine limits the development of parasites and fungi, yet does not keep them from spreading their infectious offspring everywhere throughout the body.

When a smoker quits consuming nicotine, all of a sudden these infection causing elements that have been scattered all through the body start to multiply, making an invasion in a short amount of time.

How to detox or clean body from toxins

Over the years, I have experienced family and friends dying of cancer. I observed their lifestyle and toxins they are exposed to. So to answer my friend's question on how to detox and the mechanism of cleaning our body or getting rid of toxins, I listed some items for Dos and Don'ts. Our lymphatic system which travels opposite our blood is responsible for cleaning our blood.

When we clean the many bad foods or toxins that entered our body, we must clean our liver first, our laboratory. It is closely linked to our heart that during our last breath, our liver is the first and last signal that our heart gets to shut down.

Detox or cleaning our cells from toxins is the key to living longer, the anti-aging process we all are seeking for. In my 50s, I could have died a long time ago if I was born centuries ago with no clean water, fresh produce and raising a dozen children. Each child is minus 5 years of a woman's age.

Dos in cleansing your body from toxins

- Massage
- Adequate sleep
- Filtered water
- Lemon
- Wash body with half water and half hydrogen peroxide, can be added to mouthwash too
- Baking soda (pinch in your drinking water)
- Activated charcoal
- Digestive enzymes from pineapple and papaya
- Apple cider vinegar
- Wash produce with salt or diluted vinegar
- No over ripe fruits and left over foods or 3-day old rice (aflatoxin, mycotoxin) and no charred BBQ meat
- Whole foods: sulfur-rich foods are anti-inflammatory (ginger, garlic, turmeric, coconut, walnuts)
- Deep breathing through the nose and blow out through mouth

- Prayer: May God's light energy be with you and say Amen to accept it.
- Resveratrol from Berries, kiwi, citrus fruit
- Fasting and intermittent fasting (18 hours or more)
- Activated charcoal
- Clean air

Don'ts are ways that when practiced or consumed can kill our nerve cells and produce toxins in our cells.

- Avoidance of too much caffeine, iron and sugar, these are food for cancer, parasites
- Avoid left overs, molds, fungus, parasites, uncooked meat
- Other metal toxins, trans fat, processed and plastics in food
- Stress
- Shift work, not sleeping from 10pm to 4 am
- Radiation
- Over medications, chemo, other carcinogens
- Avoid exposure to fumes, chemicals (formaldehydes, carcinogens, toxins)

If you need to lose or gain weight

Proper dietary choices combined with moderate exercise are the answer to losing or gaining weight. The food choices you make (particularly as applies to carbohydrate and oil) determine whether the body ingests foods that speed up or slow down human metabolism.

Excess consumption of simple sugars makes you fat. *Fungus* or *mold,* and *sugar* favor *fungal* and *parasite* infections.

Increased consumption of healthy oils, like flax oil, increases oxygen uptake and transport, raising metabolism and burning calories. Exercise levels and other daily activity also determine whether you will stimulate or depress your metabolism. Hours after vigorous exercise, your metabolic rate is increased. Morning exercise on an empty stomach is a more efficient way of exercising.

The Importance of Proper, Relaxed Digestion

Digestion requires more energy than any other bodily function. Processing food is the single most important bodily functions to an animal's survival, and as such, is a biological priority. Undigested food can be a place for parasites and other bad microbes to grow.

Your energy required to stay alert is temporarily diverted to digestion that you feel sleepy after a heavy meal.

Good digestion requires healthy food, a relaxed atmosphere, and thorough chewing of food. Incomplete digestion can lead to serious health problems such as creating more bad microbes (parasites).

All digested food that we use passes from our digestive system into the bloodstream. There are many ways for pathogens to enter the bloodstream—through organisms and contaminants in the foods we eat and drink, contaminated air we breathe, insect bites, cuts and other perforations of the skin, lack of sunshine, moldy foods, toxic fecal matter from birds and cats and other animals.

The digestive system is the foundation of our immune system strength. Proper gastrointestinal function is critical to adequate nutrient delivery and can impact all aspects of body function and our health.

The digestive system is designed to keep invading organisms out of our bodies.

The inside surfaces of our mouth, throat, stomach and intestines and outside surfaces make up one continuous unbroken surface

The human body's immune system is designed to attack foreign complex molecules (combinations of simple molecules) not made by our own bodies. This is one of the reasons Nature evolved our bodies to require full digestion of our foods for proper health. Bile acids have long been known to facilitate digestion and absorption of lipids in the small intestine as well as regulate cholesterol homeostasis. Bile is a complex fluid containing water, electrolytes and a battery of organic molecules including bile acids, cholesterol, phospholipids and bilirubin.

To ensure our immune system functions properly, we are designed to break down complex food groups into their smallest parts, and to later reassemble them into the more complex parts specific to our individual needs and familiar to the immune system. Complete digestion is critical to proper function of the immune system.

Partially digested food is not available to many of the body's enzymes requiring foods in their simplest form.

Undigested food can also feed other unfriendly organisms in the digestive tract. This can lead to overgrowth of yeast and bacteria leading to gas, bloating, and chronic infection. Some parasites are visually comparable to undigested foods.

The first line of defense for a healthy immune system is a healthy digestive system. Improper digestion (not chewing foods, eating uncooked meat, eating more cold foods, stress, no fiber in the diet) almost always leads to disease. We start with killing parasites and bad microbes before we nourish our bodies.

Antiparasitic herbs, digestive enzymes (pineapple and papaya), activated charcoal and fiber-rich whole foods (coconut, jackfruit, Vitamin C rich fruits) can help in reducing the number of bad microbes damaging our cells.

Relaxed digestion, constipation and losing weight

You Control Your Metabolism

How energetic you feel and what body weight or mass you maintain are determined by how you regulate your metabolism with the food and activity choices you make. Five factors affect this dramatically:

- Whole foods: Consumption of high-energy, healthy foods vs. low-energy, poor food choices with balance in minerals, fats, oils to control weight
- Calories: Total food consumed in a meal vs. energy required over the next few hours
- Exercise: Average total physical activity expended during a day

- Sleep, toxins and whole foods for proper hormone function: night time sleep, clean water, clean air, avoidance of toxins (food, environment)
- The pH balance of our bodily fluids: Ascites is the abnormal buildup of fluid in the abdomen. The mean pH of infected ascitic fluid is reported as 7.2

Vitamin C is widely distributed in all the body tissues. Its level is high in adrenal gland, pituitary gland, and retina. Its level decreases in kidneys and muscles. It is healthy to eat foods rich in Vitamin C and to supplement (ascorbates). Ascorbic acid pH is 2 and if taken with food will slightly raise the stomach's pH level. Ascorbate forms of vitamin C, which average pH 7 to 8, in high doses are best taken before meals so as not to dilute stomach acid. Supplementing with minerals is a stronger way to balance body acidity.

How to lose weight with only dieting

Your thyroid hormones play a significant role in metabolism and in energy regulation. Aerobic exercise can help boost your thyroid hormone levels. Eating more protein (cooked foods) may help boost your metabolism. A faster metabolism causes calories to be burned at a higher rate. Fasting directly impacts metabolism and the way your body uses energy. Thyroid hormones drop when in intermittent fasting. Metabolism increases during fasting of up to 48 hours. Hyperthyroid conditions have difficulty gaining weight. No fasting is recommended for those with hypoglycemia.

Nourish your body with whole foods and to go on a diet means to be careful to maintain a high nutritional content of the foods. Exercise permits efficient use of calories and oxygenates our cells. Metabolic rate is lowered with less exercise and restricted caloric intake.

1. Examine your habits, food prep, avoidance of toxins and parasites, adequate sleep, regular exercise and healthy dietary choices of whole foods (no left over, over ripe fruits, soda, unhealthy oils and sugar).

2. Avoid sugar and coffee and over ripe fruits. Eat citrus fruits and add probiotics/pickled greens and digestive enzymes (pineapple/papaya).
3. Eat whole foods before 7pm and after 10am. Eat meat during the day and no meat at night, eggs are easier to digest (30 min vs 4 hrs for meat).
4. Sleep well.
5. Use standing desk at work.
6. Prepare food during Sunday to take to work, salads and soups.
7. Add spices and try to smell cooked foods but only taste them (1–2 spoonful).
8. Chew a little longer. You can eat one good meal a day. Try low carb ketogenic diet (avocado, walnuts, coconut oil, high fiber foods).

Food pairings to lose weight

Ginger when added to fish or chicken removes the fishy smell and ginger is good for circulation. Lemon which is wealthy in vitamin C and when added to your green tea encourages absorption of nutrients from the tea. During the evening, eat healthy fats as cholesterol is synthesized around evening time.

It takes 30 minutes to digest boiled eggs however at any rate 3 hours for meat. Pineapple is rich in enzymes for efficient digestion, so eat them 30 minutes before or after a meat dish. Add vinegar as side dish or after cooking when eating greens or meats as it helps in the absorption of nutrients. Cook meat with juices of pineapple or wine to help breakdown fats. Tomatoes has vitamin C which also helps in the absorption of nutrients. Do not over cook eggs as Biotin content is decreased with cooking.

Best to eat these high-fiber fruits 30 minutes before or after eating:

✓ Avocado (6.7%)
✓ Apples (2.4%)
✓ Raspberries (6.5%)
✓ Bananas (2.6%)
✓ Carrots (2.8%)
✓ Beets (2.8%)

Cayenne and turmeric are anti-inflammatory and anti-parasitic and best eaten with meat or added in warm drink. Go for fewer calories if you are over 40 yrs. old as our digestion is slower as we age. Fiber-rich whole foods help in preventing chronic diseases. Chewing uses important enzymes in breaking down the food. Do not drink so much water while eating meat to not dilute stomach acid, important in digesting meat. Do not reheat most of the foods such as potato salad.

Fasting starves cancer cells

Intermittent fasting is scheduling eating based on cycling through periods of fasting and eating normally. Additional health benefits include promoting brain and heart health, protecting against diabetes and increasing lifespan.

Note: Studies have shed light on the role of fasting in adaptive cellular responses, to reduce oxidative damage and inflammation, to reprogram metabolic and stress resistance pathways, to optimize energy metabolism, and to bolster cellular protection. (https://doi.org/10.1016/j.cmet.2013.12.008)

optimize energy metabolism, and bolster cellular protection. In lower eukaryotes, chronic fasting extends longevity, in part, by

Periodic fasting may help you avoid mesothelioma if you're at risk for the cancer, according to new research from the University of Southern California (USC). Dr. Valter Longo, one of the authors of the USC study, explains that fasting restores the immune system by sparking creation of white blood cells.

Types of intermittent fasting include:

24-Hour Fasting. This type of fasting means not eating at all for 24 hours. Someone practicing this may choose not to eat between dinner one day and dinner the next day. This is commonly done on more than once or twice a week.

The **5:2 Diet.** The 5:2 strategy modifies 24-hour fasting. It includes limiting calories for two 24-hour periods per week. On those two days women eat 500 calories and men 600.

The **16/8 Fast.** Most popular for people using intermittent fasting to lose weight, this strategy involves not eating for 16 hours every day. Most people do this by skipping breakfast, for example, and not eating between 8:00 at night and noon the next day.

Diet which allows fruits, dairy and vegetarian friendly

Fruits contain sugars (especially over ripe ones) and vitamin C and other nutrients and fibers. Sour fruits and vitamin C-rich fruits have anti-cancer properties.

Diet which allows fruits include:

- Carb cycling: allows dairy, alcohol, considered low carb, vegetarian friendly
- Plant paradox: allows dairy, vegetarian friendly
- Intuitive eating: allows dairy, alcohol, vegetarian friendly
- Dr Grundry's diet evolution: allows dairy, alcohol, vegetarian friendly
- The Flexitarian diet:
- The Fast diet
- Dash diet
- The lose your belly diet
- The Mediterranean diet
- The MIND diet
- The SETPOINT diet
- NOOM

Calorie Restriction

This kind of eating regimen isn't actually fasting because there are no designated periods of not eating. But it is similar because it reduces overall calories. Calorie restriction includes daily calorie intake by 20 to 40 percent every day for an extended period of time. A general guideline is 1,200 calories per day for women and 1,400 for men.

Health Benefits of Intermittent Fasting

There are significant changes that happen in the body during fasting: human development hormone levels increase, insulin levels drop, cell repair procedures speed up, and there are changes to gene expression.

The benefit that most people turn to intermittent fasting for is weight loss. It is proven to promote weight loss, especially fat loss. Research is proving that there are many benefits to this style of eating that go well **beyond weight loss but also for longevity.**

It lowers blood sugar levels and helps to reduce resistance to insulin, both of which protect against diabetes. Fasting is also proven to improve cardiovascular health and to promote nerve cell growth in the brain, possibly protecting against degenerative brain diseases like Alzheimer's.

What to eat during the 8-hour feeding window, whole-8-hour

We aspire to have adequate sleep at night so that we can be productive during the day. We need the energy and motivation to stay in our healthy weight. We don't want to deprive our bodies with our favorite dish but wanted to do some cleansing to get rid of toxins we have accumulated over the years (too much alcohol, junk foods, stress, others).

If we plan to fast or not eat a heavy meal during the 16-hour period and graze or eat a good healthy meal during the 8-hour period (9am to 5pm or 10am to 6pm, 8am to 4pm), what can we do to follow this regimen to have the health we deserve without dieting but feeling our satiety and conscious of each food we chew?

1. Whole foods: We can pair plants and healthy protein, drink your favorite (1) cup of **coffee or tea during the day with ginger powder or crystals or ginger tea from fresh boiled root,** and explore more whole foods to pair with our favorite dishes.
2. Protein in the morn 9-5 ; 1 or 2 boiled eggs, boiled ginger with lemon and our favorite herbs or tea. **You can skip breakfast if you have a healthy lunch and early dinner. Fresh oranges or apples would suffice if you are doing light work and will have early healthy lunch.**

3. Apple at night, small protein (half a tsp of peanut butter). Choose bananas or fruits that are not over ripe. Create an avocado dip for your carrots or celery stick. **Apple contains 1 million good bacteria.**

4. Fibers during the day: Fiber helps encapsulate the fat and sugar out of our bodies. **Steel oatmeal (soaked first) and bitter melons are rich in fiber, help lower blood sugar and reduce fat within 6 months of daily consumption together with other healthy foods.**

5. Drink 30 minutes before full lunch and 30 minutes after lunch to not dilute the acid in the stomach.

6. Take time to chew your food, to meditate, to give thanks. Your positive spirit will guide you in nourishing your body.

7. Rest and deep breathing in between (5 minutes of rest will help you arrive at good decisions and fill up your mind with happy thoughts)

8. Love foods, healthy ones and observe the benefits derived from your food choices. Say No to unhealthy foods. Happy foods are eggs, yams and fruits.

9. Celebrate each day by noticing your good bowel movement, sleep patterns, and weighing yourself as one way of monitoring your health.

Reuse and do not reheat some foods

You can use the leftover chicken in salads or sandwich, or re-cook the chicken on the stove on a very low flame. Overheating certain cooked foods after the third day may introduce toxins such as nitrites (Alflatoxins, bacteria, etc) and can cause harm to the body.

Potatoes: How many times have you just reheated this food?

You shouldn't reheat it because it is a starchy rich food that has many health benefits. And bacteria grows in the presence of protein/foods, moisture, acidity, temperature, time to grow, and oxygen such as leftover potatoes salad with eggs and mayonnaise and not properly prepared and kept in the fridge.

When reheated it promotes the development of botulism a rare bacteria. However, it can't be killed by reheating in a microwave. It may instead lead to food-poisoning. What can you do instead? The best way is it to re-cook them in a shallow skillet.

Spinach

Popeye's favourite food is very nutritious but you must avoid reheating them. You shouldn't reheat it because: It contains a lot of nitrates which convert to nitrites when reheated, and nitrites are carcinogenic in nature. What can you do instead?

You can either eat it after steaming it or simply cool it rapidly and keep it beneath 5 degrees Celsius to prevent nitrite production.

Oil

Many times you reheat the leftover cooking oil, not realising that it can greatly harm your body. You shouldn't reheat it because you should realize that your cooking oil ought to be heated at a low fire, thereby, helping it discharge less smoke.

In case you reheat previously heated oil, it is likely to discharge toxic fumes and harmful free-radicals.What can you do instead? The best way would be to discard the oil and not re-use it. Avoid soy oil.

Beetroot

You shouldn't reheat it because beetroots just like spinach are nitrate-rich foods. Reheating them converts nitrates to nitrites which is carcinogenic to the body and can also give you a stomach ache. What can you do instead? If there's any leftovers rather than reheating it's better to eat it cold.

Rice

Rice is the most widely recognized leftover item in our kitchen and also most commonly reheated food. However, it's best to avoid reheating it in a microwave. You shouldn't reheat it because uncooked rice contains spores of bacteria and reheating it does not kill these bacteria.

In this way, if the rice is left remaining at room temperature, the pores automatically multiply. This may prove to be toxic and cause vomiting and even diarrhea. What can you do instead?

Boil water and add the leftover rice to it. Don't over-boil the rice as it would become soggy. Three-day old rice that is not refrigerated can grow aflatoxins, damaging liver cells over time.

Eggs

This staple breakfast food should not be reheated. Best known as a protein powerhouse, reheating boiled or scrambled eggs should be avoided. You shouldn't reheat it because the protein in eggs is destroyed once it's exposed to heat over and over again. Also they become toxic and unfit for consumption once they have been cooked.

Constipation, kidney stones and sedentary

A 93 yr old had hip replacement 15 years ago and lives alone. She was hospitalized due to a big kidney stones and she refused surgery. When I saw her, she has constipation for 3 days already. There are 3 medications, one is an antibiotic and aspirin for pain.

So, I warmed up her prune juice and added the following which I got her to drink as I massaged her lower back and legs and feet:

- Pinch of baking soda
- Half a tsp of apple cider vinegar (with Mother) with a pinch of turmeric
- Prune juice, warmed with pinch of brown sugar (only in small amount as parasites thrive on iron and sugar)
- 6 small slices of blueberries

She was able to defecate - have a bowel movement after the massage. I noticed that when she sits on the toilet, she is not leaning forward and the legs are far from the floor. I suggested a stool for her feet and to lean or bend forward for proper angle when using the toilet to do Number 2.

Papaya has powerful digestive enzymes, good for constipation and breaks down the coating of cancer cells so that our immune cells can easily attack them.

The massage oil is combo of many oils and the massage motion is downward motion on the lower back and on the legs. The feet has to be massaged in many different strokes with focus on the middle part and the same with the palm/hands.

Sugar: the sweet thief of life

Sugar has been a great contributor in our daily life. What contains sugar? Juice, soft drinks, etc.. Anything that isn't water contains sugar. Most of us really likes sure such as dessert. that implies we eat our very own load in sugar each year! So it may be useful to discover what that implies – what sugar truly is, the thing that sustenance esteem it has, and what issues it causes.

Sugar

White sugar is made by refining sugar cane, a process involving many chemicals. Or from beets, whose refinement also involves synthetic chemicals, and charcoal. The finished product contains none of the nutrients, vitamins, or minerals of the original plant. White sugar is a simple carbohydrate, which means a fractionated, fake.

The first plant was a simple carbohydrate which means it contained every one of the properties of an entire food: vitamins, minerals, enzymes. Refined sugar from beets and cane is sucrose. Natural fructose is not addicting and is contained in most raw fruits and vegetables. It is a natural food.

An apple contains natural sugar: fructose. A potato contains natural starch. But these are whole foods containing considerably more than just isolated carbohydrates. Apples and potatoes developed in great soil additionally contain nutrients, minerals, and proteins.

Such foods are complex carbohydrates, implying that they are complex carbohydrates, The issue comes in processed sugar and processed starch.

Whole foods prevent inflammation

Prostaglandins are the main hormones in the body that can increase or decrease inflammation. The body makes them from fatty acids. Your body produces them from the fats you ingest. Not all prostaglandins are bad, however. Your body produces two different kinds: ones that promote inflammation and ones that inhibit it. Diet to reduce pain, cyst, and other conditions such as sciatica, endometriosis, pain-related disorders

- anti-inflammatory (less pain) function
- promotes less estrogen (endometriosis and sciatica pain grows with estrogen)
- builds up the immune system what you need to include to reduce inflammation
- Your diet needs to contain fiber rich foods, lots of fruits and vegetables that will prevent constipation. Sleek fish, for example, salmon, sardines, herrings and mackerel, and halibut wealthy in omega 3 unsaturated fats.
- Moderate amounts of grass fed beef. Fresh pineapple, berries of all sorts are anti-inflammatory aid healing and also enhance the immune system.
- 2 – 3 cups of green tea per day with its fabulous anti-oxidant properties
- **Turmeric, garlic, ginger**
- The B vitamins are highly important and can be found in green peas, spinach, navy beans, nuts, pinto beans, bananas, sweet potatoes, entire grain braced oats and breads and unpolished rice and legumes. Use supplements of B1 and B12 particularly or a B complex (including all 8 B vitamins) vitamin if you are not including enough of them in your diet. B12 is needed by the body in small amounts however it is essential.
- It isn't found in plant sources (aside from seaweed) so if you do not eat any animal products at all you will need to make sure you take a good B12 supplement.
- Foods rich in Vitamins A, such as dairy products – milk, cheese and yogurt, carrots, dark green leafy vegetables, orange-coloured

fruits, (for example, mangoes and apricots, fortified margarine, eggs, mackerel and other oily fish). The beta carotene that helps the development of nutrient An in the body can be found all in all orange or yellow leafy foods however some green vegetable s where the obvious orange shade is covered up by the presence of chlorophyll. These are broccoli, apricots, carrots and sweet potatoes.

- Vitamin C is found in fruits – particularly citrus, regular and sweet potatoes, cabbage, spinach, broccoli, tomatoes, and green and yellow vegetables.
- Vitamin K sources such as broccoli and spinach, alfalfa, vegetable oils and cereals.
- Drink plenty of water. Your body needs adequate water to function at an ideal level. Adults need between 1.5 – 3 litres a day.

Unhealthy margarine, trans fat, parasites

Margarine, a man-made fat, causes an essential fatty acid deficiency, causing muscle fatigue and skin problems. Trans fatty acids block the body's production of naturally occurring anti-inflammation, adding to plaque development in the arteries and heart attacks. In 1902, the scientist Wilhelm Normann found that adding hydrogen to vegetable oil would make it solid, creating trans fats in the process

Luncheon meat, nitrosamines and cancer

Nitrites in luncheon meat becomes nitrosamines in the stomach, a carcinogen. When you do eat luncheon meat, eat it with tomatoes and Vitamin C rich foods and high fiber greens. For most people, eating remaining vegetables would not fundamentally increase the danger of cancer.

What to eat during the 8-hour feeding window, whole-8-hour

We aspire to have adequate sleep at night so that we can be productive during the day. We need the energy and motivation to stay in our healthy weight. We don't want to deprive our bodies with our favorite dish but wanted to do some cleansing to get rid of toxins we have accumulated over the years (too much alcohol, junk food, stress, others).

If we plan to fast or not eat heavy meals during the 16-hour period and graze or eat a good healthy meal during the 8-hour period (9am to 5pm or 10am to 6pm, 8am to 4pm), what can we do to follow this regimen to have the health we deserve without dieting but feeling our satiety and conscious of each food we chew?

1. Whole foods: We can pair plants and healthy protein, drink your favorite (1) cup of coffee or tea during the day, and explore more whole foods to pair with our favorite dishes.
2. Protein in the morn 9-5 ; 1 or 2 boiled eggs, boiled ginger with lemon and our favorite herbs or tea.
3. Apple at night, small protein (half a tsp of peanut butter). Choose bananas or fruits that are not over rip. Create an avocado dip for your carrots or celery stick.
4. Fibers during the day: Fiber helps encapsulate the fat and sugar out of our bodies.
5. Drink 30 minutes before full lunch and 30 minutes after lunch.
6. Take time to chew your food, to meditate, to give thanks. Your positive spirit will guide you in nourishing your body.
7. Rest and deep breathing in between (5 minute of rest will help you arrive at good decisions and fill up your mind with happy thoughts)
8. Love foods, healthy ones and observe the benefits derived from your food choices. Say No to unhealthy foods. Happy foods are eggs, yams and fruits.
9. Celebrate each day by noticing your good bowel movement, sleep patterns, and weighing yourself as one way of monitoring your health

Some processed foods such as cured meats also contain nitrate and nitrite as food additives. Some vegetables are a rich source of nitrates, but vegetables also contain ascorbic acid (Vitamin C), which is an inhibitor of nitrosamine formation. No one knows whether the vegetables' ascorbic acid completely counteracts the nitrosamine formation.

Caffeinated coffee and pure caffeine promote proteostasis – good for worms

Caffeine is implicated in many different health problems. It is a diuretic causing loss of potassium, calcium, magnesium, zinc and other minerals and B vitamins (thiamine and Vitamin C). Caffeine raised blood pressure in sensitive people. It increases the consumption of alcohol.

It over stimulates the adrenal glands causing hypo-function and fatigue. **As the population ages, there is a critical need to uncover strategies to combat diseases not related to aging but related to microbes, inflammation and other factors.**

Can a person develop an immunity to most food borne pathogens?

Parasites and infections are the two disorders for the Bolivian women, group with the longest lifespan (diet includes meat and cassava). If these food-borne pathogens overpower your body, you cannot fight them (with compromised immune system such as the young and old). Do take medications prescribed by your doctors, observing any side effects and communicating them to your doctors. Most neuro meds affect the brain and you know with the following symptoms: nausea, vomitting, dizziness and headache.

Acidic carbonated soda, bone loss and early menopause, magnesium deficiency

Carbonated beverages can cause osteoporosis.

Phosphoric acid in soda can also impair your body's ability to use other minerals, such as iron, zinc, and magnesium.

Phosphoric acid is risky on the off chance that you come into contact with it as a chemical substance. The toxic fumes can irritate your skin, eyes, and respiratory system. Carbonated water gets its fizz from carbon dioxide.

A chemical reaction in your mouth transforms the CO_2 into carbonic acid, not just giving the beverage a tangy, fiery, refreshing, yet in addition making it increasingly acidic. Most soft drinks contain caffeine, which is a nervous system stimulant that causes stress on the adrenal glands and the body, contributing to nervous stomach, anxiety, depression, high blood pressure and increased mineral loss from the body.

Even though magnesium is by far the least abundant serum electrolyte, it is extremely important for the metabolism of Ca, K, P, Zn, Cu, Fe, Na, Pb, Cd, HCl, acetylcholine, and nitric oxide (NO), for some proteins, for the intracellular homeostasis and for actuation of thiamine and therefore, for wide extent of crucial body functions.

Magnesium (Mg) absorption and disposal rely upon a very large number of variables, in any event one of which regularly goes amiss, prompting a Mg deficiency that can give numerous signs and symptoms. Furthermore, it is hindered by excess fat. Mg levels are decreased by excess ethanol, salt, phosphoric acid (soft drinks) and coffee consumption, by profuse sweating, by extreme and prolonged stress, by excessive menstrual cycle and vaginal flux, by diuretics and different medications and by specific parasites (pinworms).

The scope of pathologies related with **lack of Magnesium** is huge: hypertension (cardiovascular ailment, kidney and liver harm, and so forth.), peroxynitrite damage (headache, various sclerosis, glaucoma, Alzheimer's illness, and so on.), repetitive bacterial infection because of low levels of nitric oxide in the cavities (sinuses, vagina, center ear, lungs, throat, and so on.), fungal infections because of a depressed immune system, thiamine deactivation (low gastric behavioral disorders, and so on.), premenstrual syndrome, Calcium inadequacy (osteoporosis, hypertension, state of mind swings, and so forth.), tooth cavities,loss of hearing, diabetes type II, cramps, muscle weakening, impotence (absence of NO), hostility (absence of NO), fibromas, potassium deficiency (arrhythmia, hypertension, a few types of cancer), iron accumulation, and so on.

Salted caramelized sugar and brain opioids

Led by the College of Florida, researchers tried salted caramel on 150 fortunate members and found that when we scoff something sweet, salty or greasy, the mind discharges heroin-like chemicals called endogenous opioids.

Analysts concur that high-sugar foods can stimulate the mind similarly that medications can. Science has demonstrated that high salt foods might be addictive too. Foods like pizza and chips may stimulate opiate and dopamine receptors in the brain's reward and pleasure centers.

Can a person develop an immunity to most food borne pathogens?

Parasites and infections are the two disorders for the Bolivian women, group with the longest lifespan (diet includes meat and cassava). If these food-borne pathogens overpower your body, you cannot fight them (with compromised immune system such as the young and old).

Doctors found parasites in the brain of a senior who died of Alzheimer's disease. Wash produce with salt or diluted vinegar. Cook your meat well. Consume vinegar, cilantro and other greens. Do not go barefoot if possible. Maintain good hygiene. The world of food borne microorganisms contains a mixture of around 250 different types of bacteria, parasites, viruses, molds, and algae that are known to cause diseases in people and are therefore called food borne pathogens.

The term food-borne pathogen loosely describes the microbes that are found in animals (in farm/zoo animals and pets) and in the environment (soil, water and air) that make people sick regardless of how they became infected.

Usually, infection happens by direct ingestion of a contaminated product, but it can also happen by contact with other individuals or contact with feces from an animal (birds, cats, dogs) or pet.

Bacteria

Bacteria are the biggest group of dangerous food borne pathogens by far. They are small, one-celled microbes that come in many shapes and are capable of reproducing themselves. Cell shapes include spherical (cocci), rod-shaped (bacilli), and curved or comma-shaped (spiralled). Whether or not bacterial cells stain Gram-positive (retaining a crystal violet color) or Gram-negative (those losing the color) also aids in identifying what bacteria are present and what treatments to administer.

Viruses

Viruses are much smaller than bacteria and cannot live outside a host, such as an animal or the human body.

The two most well-known food borne viruses are Hepatitis A and Norovirus (also known as Norwalk virus). Antibiotic drugs will not help in treatment because antibiotics fight against bacteria not viruses. Take Vitamin C, zinc and eat whole foods such as ginger, pineapple, kiwi, garlic and onions to strengthen your immune system.

Parasites

There are around 20 different types of parasites known to cause disease in people from contaminated food or water. They range in size from microscopic single-celled organisms known as protozoa to visible worms known as helminthes. They get their nourishment from other living life forms known as host organism. When the parasites live and reproduce in the tissues and organs of animal and human hosts they can then be excreted in feces and go on to infect other individuals. There is a hard shell covering some varieties of protozoa that permit them to survive for lengthy periods of time in water waiting to infect another host.

Other Pathogens

There are several types of molds (fungi) that are food-borne pathogens, and algae found in plankton can cause paralytic shellfish poisoning. Mad Cow Disease, also known as Bovine Spongiform Encephalopathy (BSE), is a degenerative brain disease of cattle caused by prion particles that can be passed to humans who consume beef contaminated by the brain, spinal cord, or nervous tissue of diseased animals.

Heavy-metal contamination and synthetic plastics such as melamine have also been found in recent years to cause human illness.

Caffeinated coffee and pure caffeine promote proteostasis – good for worms

Caffeine is implicated in many different health problems. It is a diuretic causing loss of potassium, calcium, magnesium, zinc and other minerals and B vitamins (thiamine and Vitamin C). Caffeine raised blood pressure in sensitive people. It increases the consumption of alcohol. It overstimulate the adrenal glands causing hypo-function and fatigue.

Cabbage anti-cancer properties and recipes

There are numerous reasons to give cabbage a regular appearance at your meal times. It contains powerful antioxidants like vitamins A and C and phytonutrients, for example, thiocyanates, lutein, zeaxanthin, isothiocyanates and sulforaphane, which stimulate detoxifying enzymes and may ensure against breast, colon and prostate cancer. Cabbage also contains a wealth of anti-inflammatory nutrients to help hold inflammation in check.

Among them are anthocyanins, a sort of polyphenol that, as referenced, especially plentiful in red cabbage, although a wide range of cabbage contain calming polyphenols. Cabbage contains a healthy amount of B nutrients, including folate (which is superior to anything the synthetic form known as folic acid found in numerous supplements), nutrient B6, nutrient B1 and nutrient B5.

Vitamin B12 and folate in Aging: Malabsorption of the vitamin is most commonly observed as food-bound, *cobalamin* malabsorption, due to gastric atrophy in the *elderly*, and probably as a result of Helicobacter pylori infection (Lindsay Allen). Some medications cancels the absorption of folate (methotrexate, phenytoin, dilantin, phenobarbital, non-steroidal anti-inflammatory drugs).

Note: Broccoli, kale, cabbage and other crucifers, contain distinctive compounds (Sulforaphane is a sulfur-rich *compound*) that can be utilized by gut bacteria. Sulforaphane has the power to kill insects, bacteria, and worms.

- ✓ Sprouts contain 20 to 100 times more glucosinolate than mature vegetables (to protect the baby plant).
- ✓ Freezing crucifers or boiling them for 10 minutes reduces glucosinolate concentrations by about 50%.
- ✓ Steaming reduces glucosinolate concentrations by about 2/3.
- ✓ Heat completely destroys myrosinase. The bacteria in our gastrointestinal tract contain enzymes that mimic myrosinase, so sulforaphane can be generated in the process of digestion.
- ✓ About 75% of all sulforaphane in the digestive tract is absorbed into the bloodstream and taken up by cells throughout the body. Blood levels peak about 2 hours after eating crucifers.
- ✓ Once inside cells, our own natural cellular antioxidant, glutathione, rapidly binds to sulforaphane and escorts it out of cells to be eliminated within 3 hours.

EXCLI J. 2016; 15: 571–577. Published online 2016 Oct 13. doi: 10.17179/excli2016-485

- ✓ Sulforaphane (SFR) can counteract osteoporosis (Thaler el al, 2016).
- ✓ SFR protects cardiomyocytes from hypoxia (Li et al, 2016).
- ✓ SFR protects from UV damage (Sikdar et al, 2016).
- ✓ SFR slows lung cancer growth (Jiang et al, 2016).
- ✓ SFR inhibits hepatocellular carcinoma (Wu et al 2016).
- ✓ SFR has immunomodulatory effects (Pal and Konkimalla, 2016).

B vitamins are not just significant for energy, they may also slow brain shrinkage by as much as seven-overlay in brain areas explicitly known to be most affected by Alzheimer's disease.

Longevity foods, herbs and nutrients

The accompanying foods contain the best groupings of Germanium-132: broccoli, celery, garlic, Shitake mushrooms, milk, onions, rhubarb, sauerkraut, tomato juice, chlorella, all chlorophyll-rich foods and herbs such as aloe vera, ginger and ginseng.

Nutritionally, the natural element germanium has been known to help in the prevention of cancer and AIDS. Certain mixes of germanium have poisonous impacts against specific bacteria. In its organic form, germanium is being hailed as one of the best new developments in the nutritional treatment of cancer.

Numerous herbs and therapeutic plants traditionally used in healing, for example, ginseng, garlic, comfrey, and aloe–contain considerable amount of germanium. The amount of germanium in a plant varies as per the nature of the soil where it develops.

Nutrient-Drug Interactions

Nutrition can influence the body's reaction to drugs; on the other hand, drugs can influence the body's nutrition.

Foods can upgrade, delay, or lessen drug absorption. Foods disable absorption of numerous antibiotics. Grapefruit doubles the potency of medications and supplements.

They can alter drug metabolism (for example, high-protein diets can accelerate metabolism of specific drugs by stimulating cytochrome P-450. Eating grapefruit can repress cytochrome P-450 34A, easing back metabolism of certain medications (for example, amiodarone, carbamazepine, cyclosporine, certain calcium channel blockers).

A few foods influence the body's reaction to drugs. Tyramine, a segment of cheddar and a powerful vasoconstrictor, can cause hypertensive emergency in certain patients who take monoamine oxidase inhibitors and eat cheddar. Nutritional deficiencies can influence drug absorption and metabolism.

Extreme energy and protein deficiencies decrease enzyme tissue concentrations and may impair the reaction to drugs by reducing absorption or protein binding and causing liver dysfunction. Changes in the GI tract can hinder absorption and influence the reaction to a drug.

Lessons in the kitchen

As I visit seniors in their homes, I find canned foods in the kitchen and a lot of frozen processed and meat. Since my mother died, I have been researching and observing what was practiced in the kitchen that can contribute to her liver cancer. In a study about stomach cancer in 2500 Hongkong men, it was observed that dried salted fish have some bacteria in them.

We also use salted small shrimp that fermented for many years and a fish sauce. Growing up, we have ingested 3-day old rice in the absence of adequate refrigeration. **Aflatoxin in 3-day old rice was the culprit why liver cancer is the highest in the world in China.**

Tips

- Do not eat 3-day old rice, with pink molds.
- Do not eat dried salted fish that maybe too old and was not properly handled and prepared.
- Do cook fresh veggies washed with water with vinegar or salt.
- Cook your raw foods well especially meat.
- Avoid pork if you can, since the bacteria or other microbes in it multiply more compared to other meat.

Salmon with Green Apples and Pears

- Salmon
- Green apples
- Pears
- Pinch of turmeric
- Pinch of ginger
- Pinch of salt

Asparagus soup

This recipe is made with just 5, not including salt and pepper and is prepared under 25 minutes!

- 2 lbs asparagus (2 bunches), tough ends snapped off
- 1 tbsp unsalted butter
- 1 medium onion,
- chopped
- 6 cups reduced sodium chicken broth
- 2 tbsp low fat sour cream
- Kosher salt and fresh pepper, to taste

Scallion-Ginger Broth

- 1 teaspoon of vegetable oil
- 1 pinch of fresh ginger, peeled and cut to matchsticks
- 4 cups of low-sodium chicken broth
- Stir-ins (see variations), such as thinly sliced meat and vegetables, seafood, or noodles
- 4 scallions, white parts halved lengthwise and cut into 1 1/2-inch pieces, green parts thinly sliced for garnish (optional)
- 1 garlic clove, smashed and peeled
- 1 tablespoon fish sauce
- 1 tablespoon fresh lime or lemon juice

Greek Chicken with Tomatoes, Peppers, Olives, Feta

- 4 boneless, skinless chicken breast halves, cut into bite-sized pieces
- 1/4 cup flour of almond, rice, or corn of almond, rice, or corn
- 8 teaspoons Greek seasoning salt, divided, add ginger powder
- 1 teaspoon olive oil
- 1 large onion, sliced lengthwise
- 1 green pepper, cored, seeded, and sliced lengthwise into strips
- 3 Roma tomatoes, cut into eighths
- 3 tablespoons olives, chopped

Crab Salad with Grapefruit, Avocado, and Baby Greens

- 1 pink or ruby red grapefruit
- 2 tablespoons extra-virgin olive oil
- 1 tablespoon fresh lemon juice
- ¼ teaspoon granulated sugar
- ½ pound fresh crabmeat, picked over for cartilage
- 2 tablespoons chopped fresh Italian parsley
- 1 tablespoon chopped fresh chives plus additional for garnish
- Salt and freshly ground black pepper
- ½ avocado, sliced
- 4 cups (or 6.5-ounce bag) cut lettuce

Tasty Carribbean using plantain bananas

- 5-7 green bananas (plantain, boiled)
- 1/2 teaspoon salt
- 1 medium tomato
- 1 medium onion
- 1 scallion (green onion / spring onion)
- 1 clove garlic
- 1/4 habanero pepper (scotch bonnet or any hot pepper you like)
- 1 tablespoon ketchup
- 1/8 teaspoon black pepper
- 2 tablespoon olive oil (any cooking oil you like)
- 1 sprig thyme (dash dried thyme)
- Salt – optional (add as needed)
- 1 can pink salmon

Bone Broth Recipe

- beef bones (with bone marrow, white color in the middle)
- carrots
- onions
- celery
- garlic
- ginger
- bay leaves
- whole black peppercorns
- whole star anise
- cinnamon sticks
- apple cider vinegar

How to make Thai green curry with wild salmon

For the Thai green curry paste

- 1 tsp coriander seeds
- 1 tsp cumin seeds
- 1 shallot, finely chopped

- 4 green bird's-eye chillies, chopped
- 4 garlic cloves, crushed
- Thumb-sized piece fresh root ginger, grated
- 1 lemongrass stalk, finely chopped
- Pinch salt
- Small bunch fresh coriander, stalks and leaves
- 2 dried kaffir lime leaves
- 1 tbsp fish sauce
- Pinch ground white pepper

For the curry

- 1 tbsp vegetable oil
- 1 aubergine, cut into 2cm/1in chunks
- 1 x 400ml can coconut milk
- 2 tbsp Thai green curry paste (made above)
- 100g/3½oz fine green beans
- 100ml/3½fl oz chicken or vegetable stock
- 1 tbsp palm sugar, or caster sugar
- 500g/1lb 2oz raw, wild salmon
- 1 dried kaffir lime leaf
- 1 lime, zest and juice
- Small bunch fresh coriander, chopped
- Steamed jasmine rice, to serve

Cauliflower Quiche

- 1 8-ounce package frozen cauliflower
- 1 ¼ cups low-fat cheddar cheese, shredded
- ½ cup green bell pepper, cored, peeled, and chopped
- 1/3 cup onion, finely chopped
- 1 cup 1% low-fat milk
- ¾ cup egg substitute
- ½ cup biscuit mix
- ¼ teaspoon paprika
- ⅛ teaspoon pepper
- Nonfat cooking spray (avoid soy oil)

Mustard Roast Beef

- 3 tablespoons whole grain mustard
- 1 teaspoon sea salt
- 1 teaspoon freshly ground black pepper
- 3 tablespoons olive oil
- 1 1/2 tablespoons thyme leaves
- 3 cloves minced garlic and ginger
- 3 pounds boneless Rib Eye

Kale-Flaxseeds Pesto Recipe

- 1/2 bunch curly kale, thick stems removed
- 1/2 cup flaxseeds
- 2 cloves garlic
- Large pinch sea salt
- 1 tablespoon grated parmesan cheese (optional)
- Juice of 2 lemons
- 1/2 cup olive oil

Roasted Salmon and Cauliflower Rice Bowl Recipe

For the salmon

- 1 (6-ounce) piece salmon
- 1 tablespoon plus 1 tsp olive oil, divided
- small grated ginger
- 1/2 teaspoon Himalayan or sea salt, divided

For the cauliflower rice

- 1/4 head cauliflower
- 1/2 medium yellow onion, very thinly sliced
- 5 cremini mushrooms, sliced
- 1 clove garlic, minced
- 1/2 teaspoon ground cumin
- 1/4 teaspoon ground ginger

- 1/4 teaspoon ground cinnamon
- 1/4 teaspoon freshly ground black pepper
- 1/2 cup baby spinach
- Zest of 1 lemon
- 1/2 cup mixed dill, mint, and parsley leaves, roughly chopped

Lamb Burgers With Pistachio Pesto Recipe

For the burgers

- 1 ½ pounds ground lamb
- 1 teaspoon cumin
- ¼ teaspoon cinnamon
- ¼ teaspoon allspice
- grated ginger
- ½ teaspoon salt
- ¼ teaspoon black pepper
- ¼ cup mint leaves, finely chopped
- ¼ cup parsley, chopped

For the pistachio pesto

- 1 garlic clove
- 1 cup pistachios
- ½ cup coconut oil
- 1 teaspoon lemon juice, or more to taste
- ¼ cup mint leaves, loosely packed
- A pinch of salt
- Coconut Creamed Spinach With Eggs
- 2 tablespoons coconut oil, divided
- 1 pound spinach
- 1 red or yellow onion
- 1 clove garlic and grated ginger
- 1 cup coconut milk
- 2 teaspoons Dijon mustard
- Juice of 2 lemons
- 1/4 cup nutritional yeast

- 1/4 teaspoon nutmeg
- Sea salt
- Freshly ground pepper
- 5 large eggs
- Pinch cayenne pepper

Coconut with spinach and eggs, not baked

- 2 tablespoons coconut oil (used for cooking spinach and the final dish)
- 1 pound spinach (sliced in 1 inch length, cooked separately in medium heat)
- 1 onion (diced thinly, cooked separately until light brown)
- 1 clove garlic
- 1 cup coconut milk (boil separately)
- 2 teaspoons Dijon mustard
- juice of 2 lemons
- 1/4 cup nutritional yeast
- 1/4 teaspoon nutmeg
- Sea salt
- Freshly ground pepper
- 5 large eggs
- Pinch cayenne pepper
- Pinch of turmeric powder
- Pinch of ginger powder

Anti gout smoothie or juice to create an alkaline environment within your body

- 2-apples (preferably green)
- 2-pears
- 2-carrots
- 2-celery sticks
- 2-lemon (peeled)
- 1-ginger root (thumb size)
- 1-turmeric root (thumb size)

Brown Rice with Almonds

- Long grain brown rice, uncooked, 1 cup
- coconut oil, 1 tablespoon
- Onion, chopped, ¼ cup
- Garlic, 1 clove, finely chopped
- Fat-free low-sodium vegetable broth, 2 cups (chicken broth can also be used)
- Cilantro leaves, chopped, 2 tablespoons (optional)
- Ground cumin, ¼ teaspoon
- Salt, ½ teaspoon, or to taste
- Ground black pepper, ¼ teaspoon
- Slivered almonds, ½ cup

Coconut Cucumber Drink

- 33 ½ fl oz coconut water (1 container)
- 2 item(s) Persian (mini) cucumber, thinly sliced
- 4 sprig(s) fresh mint leaves (spearmint)
- 1 item(s) fresh lime(s), lime juiced
- 1 tbsp Whole Foods Market 365 Organic Light agave nectar
- 1 Tbsp ginger root, grated peeled fresh
  Note: You can use juice of ginger by boiling it in water.

Carrot Cupcakes with Cream Cheese Frosting

- Nonstick cooking spray
- 1 cup all-purpose flour of almond, rice, or corn of almond, rice, or corn
- 1 cup whole wheat flour of almond, rice, or corn of almond, rice, or corn
- ¾ cup packed brown sugar or brown sugar substitute blend equivalent to ¾ cup brown sugar (see Tip)
- 1 teaspoon baking powder
- 1 teaspoon baking soda
- ¾ teaspoon ground cinnamon
- ¼ teaspoon salt

- ¼ teaspoon ground ginger
- 2 eggs, lightly beaten
- 2 cups shredded carrots (4 medium)
- 1 cup unsweetened applesauce
- ⅓ cup coconut oil
- 6 ounces reduced-fat cream cheese (Neufchâtel)
- 3 tablespoons agave nectar or honey
- 5 tablespoons finely shredded carrot or 15 wide, very thin carrot strips

Pineapple Cupcakes

- 6 egg whites ; 3 egg yolks
- 1⅔ cups cake flour of almond, rice, or corn of almond
- ¾ cup sugar or sugar substitute blend equivalent to ¾ cup sugar (see Tip)
- 2 teaspoons baking powder
- ¼ teaspoon salt
- ½ cup unsweetened pineapple juice
- ¼ cup coconut oil ; ¼ teaspoon cream of tartar
- 2 cups thawed frozen light whipped dessert topping
- ½ cup well-drained crushed pineapple
- 2 tablespoons shredded coconut, toasted

Fruit Salad With Poppy Seed Dressing

- 8 cups fresh fruit, cut into bite-sized pieces
- 2-2/3 cups low-fat vanilla yogurt
- 1 teaspoon poppy seeds

Minted Melon Balls

- 2 cups watermelon, seedless or seeds removed
- 2 cups cantaloupe
- 2 cups honeydew melon
- 1/4 cup water
- 2 tablespoons sugar
- 2 tsp lime juice

- 3 TB fresh mint, chopped finely

Cabbage Crunch Recipe

(serves 6)

- 1/2 head red cabbage, chopped finely
- 1/2 head white cabbage, chopped finely
- 1/2 red onion, chopped
- 1/2 cup chopped cilantro
- 1/2 jalapeno pepper, minced (optional)
- For the Dressing:
- 1 teaspoon gomasio (ground sesame with salt)
- 1 cup almond butter
- 1/2 cup cilantro, chopped
- 1 tablespoon toasted sesame oil
- 1 tablespoon minced fresh ginger
- 1/2 jalapeno pepper, chopped (optional)
- Juice of half a lemon
- 1 tablespoon apple cider vinegar
- 1 tablespoon seasoned rice vinegar
- 1 cup olive oil
- 1 tablespoon white miso paste* (optional)

White sesame pudding

- 400 ml coconut milk, soy milk and almond milk
- 4 tbsp white sesame paste
- 45 grams soft light brown sugar
- 8 grams powdered gelatin
- 1 mixed seeds (optional)

Coconut chia seed pudding

- 1 can coconut milk (approx. 13.66 oz can)
- 1 tablespoon coconut nectar (liquid coconut sugar) optional
- 1/3 cup chia seeds

QUESTION AND ANSWERS

Can the health of our gut predict disease and lifespan?

A healthy cell must have sufficient nutrient and healthy environment to work with vitality. Sleep, whole foods, exercise, sunshine, and absence of bad microbes (virus, parasites, bacteria, fungus). With poor immune system, presence of bad microbes in the gut, lack of sleep, poor diet and stress can facilitate the growth of cancer and other disease related to aging (Alzheimer's, etc). The microbiome, mix of microbes in the gut, can anticipate our risk of dying within 15 years (Biology, health doi:10.1126/science.abb0111).

Why are cancers treated by origin (ex: lung, breast, brain, etc.) instead of by mutation or signaling pathways?

Because our medicine is categorized by specialty: lung specialist, endocrinologist, neurologist, so on.

Adenocarcinoma is equal colon cancer, pancreatic cancer, lung cancer, stroke, and other cancers that cannot be detected by MRI. Because it is hormonal in origin and its course is 2 months (death happens quickly) but it started 20 yrs ago from indigestion and exposure to toxins (turns off/on our genes).

Is cancer increasing in the U.S.?

Metabolic related cancer (from processed foods, lifestyle) and environmental toxins can increase the incidence of cancer in the USA and around the world.

Statistics: The Weight of Cancer in the U.S

In 2018, an expected 1,735,350 new instances of cancer will be diagnosed in the US and 609,640 individuals will die from the sickness.

The most well-known cancer (recorded in slipping request as per assessed new cases in 2018) are breast cancer, lung and bronchus cancer, prostate cancer, colon and rectal cancer, melanoma of the skin, bladder cancer, non-Hodgkin lymphoma, kidney and renal pelvis cancer, endometrial cancer, leukemia, pancreatic cancer, thyroid cancer, and liver cancer.

The quantity of new instances of cancer (cancer growth rate) is 439.2 per 100,000 people for every year (in view of 2011–2015 cases).

The quantity of cancer deaths (cancer mortality) is 163.5 per 100,000 people for each year (in view of 2011–2015 deaths).

Cancer mortality is higher among men than women (196.8 per 100,000 men and 139.6 per 100,000 women).

When looking at gatherings dependent on race/ethnicity and sex, malignancy mortality is most elevated in African American men (239.9 per 100,000) and least in Asian/Pacific Islander women (88.3 per 100,000).

In 2016, there were an expected 15.5 million cancer survivors in the US.

The quantity of cancer survivors is relied upon to increment to 20.3 million by 2026.

Roughly 38.4% of people will be determined to have cancer growth sooner or later during their lifetimes (in view of 2013–2015 information).

In 2017, an expected 15,270 kids and teenagers ages 0 to 19 were determined to have diagnosed with cancer and 1,790 died because of it.

Same with every one. At age 80, 1 in every 3 women can be prone to cancer in the USA when living the American lifestyle.

Why are lung, skin, and colon cancer so common?

Invasion of inflammatory toxins that harm our immune system. First our liver is bombarded with toxins and the effect is shown in the health of our skin.

Colon cancer is greatly affected when our metabolism is not healthy as we eat more processed foods.

What is stopping cancer from being cured?

Identifying cancer in late stage, stage 4 and some cancer hide in many organs and cells such as endocrine cancer. Presence of E. Coli and other infectious agents, poor metabolism, aging, low immune function and exposure to other carcinogens can be an environment to promote cancer growth. Here cancer and invading pathogens (parasites) are one and the same.

Is it possible to distinguish cancer symptoms that clinical investigations did not recognize?

Yes. Signs are: skin itching, chronic cough for over 4 years, low platelet, PSA values, knee or back pain, blood test results on blood glucose, lipids, etc. not getting adequate sleep check for eye and skin health lose of appetite and loss of weight.

Is cancer a genetic or inflammatory disease?

Metabolic 80%, Genetic 20%

Would it be advisable to stress over lung cancer at the age of 21?

Use the power of your mind to stop smoking. Carcinogens from cigarettes smoking in due time will accumulate to lead to lung cancer, the most painful cancer of all. Increase your intake of Vitamin C and amino acid lyceine. Always ensure that your immune system is strong with exercise, eating whole foods (cilantro and other greens/bitters/colored veggies) and getting good sleep. Take probiotics and eat citrus/pineapples. CAT scan and MRI scan can detect lung cancer. But at your age, concentrate on stopping smoking.

How does lung cancer heal?

Vitamin C, amino acid lyceine, sulfur rich foods, greens such as cilantro for metal detox, sleep, lemon in water, ketogenic diet.

Has anyone determined what number of cigarettes it takes to execute an individual, state in 1 year?

Smoking a parcel of cigarettes daily prompted:

- 150 mutations in each lung cell every year
- 97 in the larynx or voice box
- 23 in the mouth
- 18 in the bladder
- six in the liver

A person has 3rd stage lung disease, what are the odds of survival?

It depends on your immune system and the severity of the cancerous cells. Find some doctors who knew new therapies such as immunotherapy for lung cancer. Take Vit C, prebiotic and probiotic, digestive enzymes, turmeric and ginger, wash back with salt and hydrogen peroxide, amino acid Lysine, tea of lemon grass, whole foods (red colors containing resveratrol - plums, grapes,walnuts)

How can a vaccine prevent lung cancer?

One approach to cancer vaccination is to separate proteins from cancer cells and immunize patients against those proteins, in the hope of stimulating the immune system to kill the cancer cells. Research on cancer vaccines is underway for treatment of breast, lung, colon, skin, kidney, prostate and other cancers.

Utilizing immunizations in the treatment of malignant growth is generally new, in any case, and mostly exploratory.

Helpful immunizations for bosom, lung, colon, skin, renal, prostate, and different malignancies are presently being explored in clinical preliminaries.

Can anxiety cause stomach pain?

Yes, it can also cause arthritis pain and other inflammation. Our diet is unique for each of us and should be adjusted towards healthy foods and lifestyle to account for age, gender, race, income, marital status and medication use (most medications are acidic). Chronic anxiety is one of the symptoms of Parkinson's disease.

Some parasites (toxoplasma gondii) causes generalized anxiety. Seropositivity for T gondii was associated with 2.25 times greater odds after adjusting for age, gender, race, income, marital status and medication use (Markovitz AA, et al. Brain Behav Immun. 2015).

Nocturnal worms, sundowning in seniors with mental health issues

Alcohol, caffeine, nicotine, herbs and vegetables are natural pesticides. Addictive substances can be natural pesticides or pain killers. Alcohol is metabolized to vinegar which inhibit worms. Worms and humans are natural nocturnals, eating at night as hunger is present. Feed nocturnal catfish before turning off the light. Seniors must eat at 7pm before going to bed (1-2 hours before turning off the lights) to prevent sundowning.

Oils to prevent insect bites and parasitic worms

Mix any of these oil in base of almond or coconut oil:

✓ Citronella oil
✓ Eucalyptus oil
✓ Garlic oil
✓ Lavender oil
✓ Pennyroyal
✓ Peppermint oil
✓ Rosemary oil
✓ Tea tree oil
✓ Oregano oil
✓ Lemongrass oil
✓ Baobab oil
✓ Ginger oil
✓ Bay leaf oil
✓ Sage oil

What changes would one be able to make in their way of life to better their odds against cancer?

Causes: EMF, cancer causing substances, hormone disrupting plastics, X-rays, smoking, medications,drugs and other lifestyles that disrupts or lead to epigenetic changes to our DNA and other multifactorial causes.

Exercise and nature walks

Whole foods and avoidance of toxins. Some powerful detoxifiers are cilantro,lemon,aloe, parsely, greens and red colored veggies. Sleep and de-stress to detox. Our brain detoxes during sleep (following normal rhythms of day and night). Beware of side effects from medications, drugs and other toxins Avoid plastics, toxins, carcinogens, sugar, trans fat, charred BBQ meat and other tips .

Can hypothyroidism become cancer?

Hypothyroidism is an underactive thyroid gland resulting in retardation of growth and insufficient amount of hormone that slows life-sustaining body processes, damages organs and tissues throughout the body, and can result in life-threatening complications. Most older women have hypothyroidism, making them more likely to have cancer at end stage.

Has cancer been found to be man made?

Carcinogens abound or surround us. Triclosan in our mouth wash, charred meat from BBQ, plastics, parasites, animal feces, molds, fungus, air pollution, chemical toxins, contaminated water, aging, stress, lack of sleep, inflammation, infection, over medication and other unknowns.

What number of women endure ovarian cancer at stage 3/4?

Depends on the age of the person. The immune system is stronger when we are younger. Vitamin C can help.

Are certain parts of the body more inclined to create tumors?

Why? Fat tissues in breasts and prostate are sensitive to carcinogens and toxic substances settle in fat tissues. Endocrine Destroying substances (plastics) affect our hormonal balance. Air pollution, chemical fumes, weak immune system and metal toxins are contributing factors in lung cancer. Genetic data for these 3 cancers are well identified. Assumption: Female/Male, over 50yrs of age, on western diet, lives in Northern hemisphere, have families with cancer, diabetes and polyps, prone to allergies (lack zinc), digestive disorders, high dairy and sugar consumption (low magnesium and calcium,iron) and had utilized a few drugs before.

Any reasons of prostate cancer in men?

COPKL: Colorectal, ovarian/uterine, prostate, kidney, liver and bladder cancer risk Factor. Assumption: Female/Male, over 50yrs of age, on western diet, lives in Northern hemisphere, have families with cancer, diabetes and polyps, prone to allergies (lack zinc), digestive disorders, high dairy and sugar utilization (low magnesium and calcium,iron) and had utilized a few drugs before.

COPKL Risk Factor = Blood sugar (0.2) + history (0.1) + sugar/processed foods consumption (0.1) + Exercise and sun exposure (0.1) + number of medications (0.1) + obesity/night time worker (0.1) + exposure to copper,fungus,molds,aflatoxins (0.1) + genes (0.2) COPKL Risk Factor =1.0 (High) COPKL Risk Factor = 6- 4 (Medium)

Is there any logical proof that any food has anti-cancer benefits?

Yes, the allium or garlic family. The bitter greens. Sulfur rich foods. Cilantro family and more.

What are the best ways to prevent cancer?

- Exercise, sufficient sleep, social volunteering functions
- Nurture (massage, yoga,nature walks, dancing,playing music)
- Avoidance of environmental **toxins/parasites/molds/fungus/chemical fumes/endocrine disrupting hormones-chemicals/**

metal toxins from birth to old age, breastfeeding,homebirth,less use of medications, no smoking, less use of alcohol and maintaining a normal weight, processed foods,avoidance of air pollution

- Constant monitoring of body functions (comprehensive blood work,labs) and signs (headache, pain,chronic cough, skin discoloration) and communicating to doctors about these signs early - not waiting to lead to chronic stage.

Do you think cancer is man-made and to profit and populace control?

Man made toxins in the environment, ingested or exhaled can affect our cells from growing and some animals (sharks) get cancer too. We detox with sleep, whole foods and exercise. Some medications increase the growth of cancer cells and causes other diseases such as Parkinson's and Alzheimer's disease. Prevent cancer with a stronger immune system (Vitamin C, Echinacea tincture,zinc, whole foods, Vitamin D, happy disposition) and clean water,air and food supply (wash veggies with salt and diluted vinegar).

How did you discover that you have cancer?

My father's lung cancer was identified using an MRI and CAT scan and was in the last stage, stage 4. A complete DNA sequence tests can ID cancer too.

Could another medication combination cause cancer to eat itself?

Cancer is often treated with some combination of radiation therapy, surgery, chemotherapy, and targeted therapy. Doctors are using genetics, cancer chemotherapy and many other combination of treatment since they know that they have to be precise and target cancer in many areas. In some studies, Vitamin C helps fight cancer by breaking down into hydrogen peroxide, which can damage tissue and DNA. The new study shows that tumor cells with low levels of catalase enzyme activity are much less capable of removing hydrogen peroxide than normal cells, and are more susceptible to damage and death when they are exposed to high doses of vitamin C. A mixed of immune T cells can kill cancer but not all of them. These cancer-killing T cells are defined by the standard receptor that T cells normally use to recognize infected cells (Nature Immunology, 2020. DOI: 10.1038/s41590-0`9-0578-8).

For what reason is there an inverse relationship among cancer and Alzheimer's disease?

Alzheimer when not severe is just normal aging. Inflammation (caused by stress, infection, parasites, toxins, lack of sunshine, lack of sleep and other multifactorial causes) and lack of greens (whole foods, Vitamin C, probiotic, prebiotic) in the diet are possible factors causing Alzheimer's.

Is it genuine that there are individuals who switched or restored cancer through nutrition?

Yes. Depending on the severity of cancer cells, early stage can be cured by Vitamin C and amino acid Lysine rich foods and supplements (for lung cancer). Any supplementation or nutrition cannot help during the last stage of cancer (true for my father) because he already started with weak immune system. Nutrition is only one of the 5 ways for early stage cancer to heal: immune system, lifestyle (avoidance of toxins), detox (nutrition,others), emotional state (social support), current physical strength/stamina/health.

What are the most common age related diseases?

Cancer, infections from parasites, bacteria and virus and organ damage. Eating less meat or methionine-rich foods slows aging. Sleeping at night helps us detox our cells from toxins. Parasites invade our cells and weakens our organs especially vulnerable during old age, and the end product is cancer (grows over time, at least for 20 years). Over exposure to air pollution and unclean water kills our lungs and hearts.

What might happen to the mind if you forced yourself to learn all day long for a long time?

Brain needs 8 or more hours of night time sleep to detox your body. Lack of sleep, unhealthy liver and alcohol age the body in a faster way. A graduating civil engineer student has to study and complete his assigned drawings for 3 consecutive days without sleep while soaking his feet in water to keep awake. He died on the third day.

How beneficial is Apple cider vinegar for an individual's liver?

Apple cider vinegar can clean your house and your body. It is high in acetic acid, with strong natural effects and can kill many types of harmful bacteria. It lowers blood sugar levels, blood pressure and fights diabetes and helps you lose weight and reduces belly fat.

Does early onset Alzheimer's disease progress faster when diagnosed in the early 50's as opposed to the 70's?

This is what I observed in care homes. I learned that gut metabolism influences our brain function. And as we age, we are more prone to cancer and other chronic health issues. Our tissues are not stronger allowing other microbes to travel and harm our bodies. A stronger immune system is what we need.

How do our cells age?

We age when microbes over power our good cells, turning against us. When this happens, they contribute to lack of sleep while they consume our nutrients. Our brain is not getting help in cleaning up toxins in our body which happens during deep night time sleep. We spend less time in movement or cardio-based exercises like walking or jogging, not getting sunshine and clean air and water. We are busy being stressed out and have anxiety as gut microbes are not balanced and our adrenals and liver cannot keep up with the tasks of getting rid of toxins in our body.

Physical activity or exercise purges the blood of a substance which accumulates during stress and can be harmful to the brain.

Why have endocrinological diseases like diabetes, thyroiditis, etc. become so common these days?

Stress is the appropriate response with the majority of us not sleeping and not getting continuous 9 hours rest. Adrenals and liver come to the rescue as blood sugar levels drop. The endocrine pancreas, liver and adrenal glands work to normalize blood sugar and triglycerides.

Take care of your stress so it will be easier for you to prevent obesity, depression, sugar cravings and nerve pain which may start to happen at around 45-55 years of age. When we take care of our stress level, we take care of our metabolism, brain, whole body and we then prevent chronic diseases that lead to cancer and other inflammation (Alzheimer, Parkinson, ALS, etc).

Activities to make you happy

Beach stroll, dancing, watching comedians, laughing, sleeping at nigh, massage, happy and loving friends and relationships, spending time with family and friends, playing with your pets, gardening, singing, praying, deep breathing exercise, meditation

Side effects of chronically elevated cortisol can include:

Anxiety, Autoimmune diseases, Cancer, Chronic fatigue syndrome, Common Colds, Hormone imbalance, Irritable bowel disease, Thyroid conditions, Weight loss resistance

Needed nutrients

Digestive enzymes, vitamin C (citrus, kiwi, berries, tamarind), vitamin B, L-carnitine, chromium, anti-oxidants, fiber-rich foods (squash, yams, sulfur family of garlic and onions, greens, okra, radish), spearmint, ginger, beets, carrots, all root crops, sprouts, pineapple, papaya, taurine rich foods (breastmilk, sea algae, fish)

- Eleuthero ginseng
- Holy basil
- Rodiola rosea
- ashwagandha
- Astralagus
- Sour date
- Mimosa pudica: Extracts of Mimosa pudica are effective in clearing out hurtful microbes and can be valuable in antibacterial items
- Medicinal mushrooms: Mushrooms are wealthy in B nutrients, for example, riboflavin (B2), folate (B9), thiamine (B1), pantothenic corrosive (B5), and niacin (B3).
- Licorice root
- Valerian

Is there an evidence that can support of Alzheimer's disease increasing the porosity of the blood-brain barrier?

Microbes that was not detoxed during sleep causing memory tangles because they traveled via the vagus nerve creating memory tangles that leads to Alzheimers. The person has excess blood sugar and the body is aging faster.

What are some great exercises for early to mid-stage dementia patients with poor visual perception?

- sitting exercise
- listening to music
- tactile activities: wiping, cleaning
- being in group
- getting sunshine, in wheelchair
- learning new skills without the need for clear vision
- **What can a 60 year old women do to lose pounds?**
- Start with detox

- Adequate sleep, probiotics, more sulfur rich foods such as turmeric, ginger and garlic
- Walking, massage
- Being happy

What happens in the mind when it gets a lot of dopamine for a long period of time?

Safeguard your brain's pleasure centres. Profound inside the openings of the cerebrum are structures associated with joy and inspiration, most notably two areas called the nucleus in the left and right hemisphere.

They are seriously activated by the neurotransmitter dopamine with substances like cocaine, sex, computer games, high-fat, sugary food, and fame.

Dopamine fuels addiction, making everyday activities less interesting. Intense pleasure means huge dopamine dumps, which over time causes the nucleus accumbens to be less responsive, consequently causing the need for more and more of the behaviours.

You can protect your pleasure centres by limiting thrill-seeking activities that could wear them out, like racing, cocaine, Methamphetamines, excessive video games, pornography, and scary movies.

Rather, engaging in safer behaviors that protect the mind, for example, daylight, exercise, meditation, and tuning in to pleasurable music, can help cushion your pleasure centres. Having a dedicated passion and purpose in life also helps to activate the pleasure centres in a healthy way.

How can we reverse autoimmune conditions?

- We clean our gut microbes and take in more whole foods rich in Vitamins D sunshine, E, C (citrus) and A, all important for healthy skin. Fibromyalgia in women is associated with alteration in gut microbiome.
- Newborns have stronger immune system promoted by breastmilk, massage and loving care.
- There are cleansing herbs such as ginger, turmeric, and the sulfur family like asparagus, garlic and onions.

- Adequate sleep helps us detox.
- Take care of your liver by avoiding alcohol and over medicating.
- Avoidance of environmental toxins which can lead to interstitial lung disease (ILD)

There are also many known reasons for ILD, including:

- Autoimmune diseases (in which the immune system assaults the body, for example, lupus, rheumatoid joint pain, sarcoidosis, and scleroderma
- Lung inflammation because of taking in a foreign substance, for example, certain types of gas, fungus, or mold (hypersensitivity pneumonitis)
- Medicines, (for example, nitrofurantoin, sulfonamides, bleomycin, amiodarone, methotrexate, gold, infliximab, and etanercept)

Why is interstitial fluid pressure elevated in tumors?

Tumors or cancer cells invasion.Stronger immune system in alkaline body ph helps such as drinking water with baking soda, Vit C, B and omega 3, adequate sleep and avoid stress/sugar/toxins.

What food exacerbates inflammatory response if you are arthritic?

- Fried and processed
- Fried and processed foods
- AGEs. Lower your AGEs
- Sugars and refined carbs. Sugars and refined carbs
- Dairy. Dairy products
- Alcohol and tobacco
- Salt and preservatives
- Corn oil

How to differentiate from viral cold or bacterial virus?

Cold starts as a viral and then when the immune system is so weak, bacteria can invade the body. Bacterial infection is yellow,green,rust-colored,or bloody mucus that is coughed up from the lungs,especially while other symptoms are getting worse.

Can someone workout when you have anemia?

Yes, just bring this food to chew/eat in the morning: soft boiled eggs, raisin, dark chocolate, rosemary, oregano, nuts, small seeds, figs, molasses syrup, liver pate, and homemade lemonade with maple syrup and choco.

What is the difference between a person with high metabolism and with low metabolism?

Low metabolism will have stronger side effects from medications while high metabolism have more side effects from medications, absorbs more nutrients, does not get drunk from alcohol easy, do not have allergies and have stronger immune system.

Does excess dietary calcium increase dementia risk, and if so, are there countermeasures that can be taken for this?

Free calcium (from processed foods and TUMS) can be detoxed by ingesting vitamins and minerals, eating whole foods like cilantro, exercise, adequate sleep and other holistic ways.

What can I do to help my grandma who has Alzheimer's?

Be a caregiver, companion and do some activities together. Prepare ketogenic diet. Exercise together as you count together. Sunshine, fresh air, clean water and whole foods with massage will help her.

Do most people get Alzheimer's disease and if so should they not learn anything new?

Only 25% of seniors get Alzheimer's disease, 3x more with women, who are over stressed, hormonal imbalance, on meat diet with processed foods/toxic food, do not exercise, on sugary and toxic diet and has genetic predisposition (15% contribution).

Alzheimer's/Dementia is type 3 diabetes. It has metabolic origin, related to gut health (bad bacteria in the gut, can be controlled by probiotics and whole foods and avoidance of trans fat and sugar).

Delirium occurs after surgery or hospitalization or seeing a doctor, lowers the immune system and doubles the progression of Dementia/Alzheimer's disease.

Some medications such as antipsychotics, tramadol and Benzodiazepam, can cause dementia and parkinson's.

Why is Alzheimer's significant to feminism?

The ratio of women getting Alzheimer's to men is 3:1. At old age, most women are single or widowed as men die early (5 years early than women). So women are at the mercy of family members, government health care and friends to be with them during old age. Lifestyle and environment affect how long a woman lives.

What's the point in learning anything if most people just get Alzheimer's disease?

Living life, feeling the adrenaline rush when learning new things, finding enjoyment and this life is worth living for because of everything we learned, experienced and enjoy. Only 25% gets Alzheimer's and most of them reach the age of 100 without any symptoms.

What is my dad's genetic risk of getting a neurodegenerative disease?

10–20%

What is the no 1 challenge for people caring for a relative with Alzheimer's?

Time and manpower. We need caregivers 24/7. At times depending on level of care that is needed, it is a 24/7 care.

Do most people get Alzheimer's disease before they're 30?

No, more after 85

Is there any beneficial diet for a person with dementia or Alzheimer?

Whole foods rich in sulfur, grapes, garlic, pickled greens and fish/nuts for omega 3/EFA.

If I am smart and have great cognitive reserves, does it prevent or delay Alzheimer's? Does it prevent or delay vascular dementia?

Yes. Use your brain or lose your it. But remember that mental health is also affected by our gut microbiome, so add probiotics, pickled veggies or acidophilus in your diet/supplements. Avoid stress. Vitamin B complex and sleep can lessen it. Sleep more. Exercise your body to grow your neurons. Get sunshine, walk in nature or take Vitamin D3. And eat more whole foods or a low carbs ketogenic diet.

All the above will help you especially when you avoid drugs (include smoking and alcohol) or medications that affect your brain (narcotics,prescribed or OTC).

If vaccines do cause autism, would you still give you and your children vaccines?

After I read the book on vaccination, I changed the schedule from 12mon start instead of 2 months. My first born had vaccination at 2months and my second at 12months start. Scientist said that the formaldehyde in the vaccine is very minimal.

How much physical activity is too much?

Listen to your body. Boys are supposed to start sports only after they reach the age of 14 (developed bones are ready by then). I suggest to take it slow as there are many more years you have to care for your body.

Is combining medications, nutrition, thinking and behavioural changes the psychiatry of the future?

Yes. Our mental health is influenced by our gut microbiome. Our nervous system when weak leads to weak immune system and also unhealthy gut microbiome. And that many whole foods are happy foods, sources of dopamine and many important neurotransmitter. Yoga, music, exercise, volunteering and whole foods can greatly impact our mental health.

What are alternative health ways to treat chronic abdominal nerve pain after all traditional methods have failed?

Vitamin B complex, adequate sleep, probiotics, baking soda, digestive enzymes, turmeric, ginger, sauna, sunshine

Is there anything I can do to reduce the odds of dementia or Alzheimer's?

- learning new skills
- probiotics, kill or prevent parasites, fungus, molds and bad bacteria from overpowering our good bacteria//microbes
- more veggies (greens, green plantain banana, sweet potatoes, soft boiled eggs) than red meat, alcohol, caffeine, sugar, soda and other processed foods
- exercise in the sun
- adequate sleep
- hydration with citrus/calamansi/lime/kiwi/spearmint/pineapple/blueberries

Is there a particular food that is more healthy than any other?

Sour fruits and bitter greens, purslane leaves, dandelion leaves, pineapple, apples, kiwi, garlic, ginger and blueberries

What are non-genetic factors that can cause chronic diseases?

Environmental toxins contribute to toxins in our body.

Aging makes us 10,000 times more prone to cancer. Iron metabolism dysfunction can affect tumor progression.

Our genes affect our health 20% of the time but can be reversed with healthy lifestyle.

What is worst, labor pains in the back or pains in the stomach?

Back labor pain is where the baby is facing your back. Be on hands and knees position to offload the baby's weight and have a warm compress on your lower back. Before labor, do walk on the stairs to position baby's head at right position.

What is a simple anti aging skin care regime?

Hydration, sun block, adequate sleep, vitamin E and C homemade face cream and wash face with water with citrus or tsp of vinegar and or hydrogen peroxide

Can disordered or poor sleep in your 50s and 60s increase Alzheimer's disease risk?

Yes, during sleep we detox. Memory tangles means we were not able to clean our toxins in the brain.

Can antioxidants help with hangovers?

Yes for antioxidants before you drink and eating protein while drinking alcohol. Factors That Affect How Alcohol is Absorbed Did you realize, given the same exact amount of alcohol, the level of intoxication varies according to some physiological and biological factors? Here are some examples:

1. Biological Sex
    All in all, alcohol is utilized at an alternate rate in women than it is in men. This is due to general differences in body composition.

Studies have also demonstrated that women have less of the prot]eins used to use alcohol than men do (alcohol dehydrogenase and acetaldehyde dehydrogenase). Google women alcohol metabolism. See https://alcohol.stanford.edu/alcohol-drug-info/i-bet-you-didnt-know/metabolism

2. Weight Body

Weight determines the amount of space through which alcohol can diffuse in the body. When all is said in done, an individual who gauges 180lbs will have a lower blood alcohol focus than a 140lb individual who drank a similar sum.

3. Medications

Other drugs and medications can have adverse effects and unpredictable interactions with alcohol. Even Tylenol can cause significant liver troubles if paired with alcohol.

Make a point to know what the potential interactions with medications/drugs you have taken before you drink. In some cases, these interactions can be fatal. When in doubt, don't drink alcohol when taking meds since it **potentiates (doubles the potency)** the meds or even supplements. See https://www.rxlist.com/drug-interaction-checker.htm

4. Drinking on an empty stomach vs. eating while you drink

Drinking on an empty stomach irritates your digestive system, and results in more rapid absorption of alcohol. Do eat high-protein foods (eggs, tofu, nuts, beans, cheese) alongside alcohol previously and when drinking, and you'll abstain from getting too drunk.

5. Health Concerns

Genetic enzyme deficiencies (alcohol dehydrogenase and aldehyde dehydrogenase), diabetes, hypertension, thiamine deficiency, depression, seizure disorder and a myriad of other health conditions may decrease the body's ability to process alcohol and therefore present increased health risks.

Alcohol and other drug dependencies may increase the risk of developing chronic disease and long-term dependence. Consult with your health care clinician.

6. "Chugging" vs. "Skillful sipping"

Why does chugging significantly increase the chances of unwanted risks? Going overboard with drinking is like overdosing. The more alcohol you drink inside a brief time frame, the more you exhaust your body's capacity to use the alcohol.

It responds by shutting down. First, your cognitive system shuts down, your inhibitions are lowered and your motor functioning is significantly impaired.

Pour in more alcohol, and your body might force you to vomit (first sign of alcohol poisoning), or pass out (other brain functions shut down). Finally, your sympathetic and parasympathetic systems will shut down due to systemic alcohol poisoning. Enjoy your drink more slowly and spread your drinking out over time and you can control how intoxicated you become.

Note: There, an enzyme known as alcohol dehydrogenase (ADH) converts ethanol into acetaldehyde, a toxic byproduct which the body quickly eliminates using another enzyme called ALDH. Alcohol metabolism in the body. Ethanol is converted to acetaldehyde by the ADH enzymes (yellow).

What are the organic products that I should drink to have a more beneficial hair, and how frequently in seven days would it be advisable for me to drink it?

Skin and hair health are the same. Nutrients for both are Vitamin A, B, C and E. My son has the same problem. Eat raw or soft boiled eggs rich in Biotin. Massage hair with coconut oil before showering, cold water for hair (every other day). Less stress, sleep more and whole foods diet.

What happens to the brain when it gets an excessive amount of dopamine for a significant lot of time?

Safeguard your brain's pleasure centres. Profound inside the openings of the cerebrum are structures required with delight and inspiration, most outstandingly two territories called the core accumbens in the left and right hemisphere.

They are seriously initiated by the synapse dopamine with substances like cocaine, sex, computer games, high-fat, sugary foods, and fame. Dopamine fuels addiction, making everyday activities less interesting. Intense pleasure means huge dopamine dumps, which over time causes the nucleus accumbens to be less responsive, consequently causing the need for more and more of the behaviors.

You can protect your pleasure centres by limiting thrill-seeking activities that could wear them out, like racing, cocaine, Methamphetamines, excessive video games, pornography, and scary movies. Rather, captivating in more secure practices that ensure the brain, for example, daylight, exercise, contemplation, and tuning in to pleasurable music, can help cushion your pleasure centres. Having a dedicated passion and purpose in life also helps to activate the pleasure centres in a healthy way.

What is the best nutrition?

Whole foods eaten with proper chewing, less stress, deep breathing, adequate sleep, fresh air, clean water and exercise.

Is an individual's metabolic rate related to aging?

Age is one of the most important factors of changes in energy metabolism.

The basal metabolic rate decreases almost linearly with age.

Skeletal musculature is a fundamental organ that consumes the largest part of energy in the normal human body. The total volume of skeletal muscle can be estimated by 24-hours creatinine excretion.

The volume of skeletal musculature decreases and the percentage of fat tissue increases with age. It is shown that the decrease in muscle mass relative to total body may be wholly responsible for the age-related decreases in basal metabolic rate. Energy consumption by physical activity also decreases with atrophic changes of skeletal muscle.

Energy requirement in the elderly decreases. With decrease of energy intake, intake of essential nutrients also decreases. If energy intake, on the other hand, exceeds individual energy needs, fat accumulates in the body. Body fat tends to accumulate in the abdomen in the elderly.

Fat tissue in the abdominal cavity is connected directly with the liver through the portal vein.

Accumulation of abdominal fat causes disturbance in glucose and lipid metabolism. It is shown that glucose tolerance decreases with age. Although age contributes independently to the deterioration in glucose tolerance, the decrease in glucose tolerance may be partly prevented through changes of lifestyle variables, energy metabolism is essential for the physiological functions.

It may also be possible to delay the aging process of various physiological functions by change of dietary habits, stopping smoking, and physical activity.

How does sugar cause aging?

Sugar is bad for our liver. Red wine and other beverages have sugar.

Insufficient hepatic O2 in animal and human studies has been shown to elicit a hepatorenal reflex in response to increased hepatic adenosine, resulting in the stimulation of renal as well as muscle sympathetic nerve activity and activating the renin angiotensin system.

Low hepatic ATP, hyperuricemia, and hepatic lipid accumulation reported in metabolic syndrome (MetS) patients may reflect insufficient hepatic O2 delivery, potentially accounting for the sympathetic overdrive associated with MetS.

This theoretical concept is supported by experimental results in animals fed a high fructose diet to induce MetS.

Hepatic fructose metabolism rapidly consumes ATP resulting in increased adenosine production and hyperuricemia as well as elevated renin release and sympathetic activity.

This review makes the case for the hepatorenal reflex causing sympathetic overdrive and metabolic syndrome in response to exaggerated splanchnic oxygen consumption from excessive eating.

This is strongly reinforced by the fact that MetS is cured in a matter of days in a significant percentage of patients by diet, bariatric surgery, or endoluminal sleeve, all of which would decrease splanchnic oxygen demand by limiting nutrient contact with the mucosa and reducing the nutrient load due to loss of appetite or dietary restriction.

Do dementia/Alzheimer's patients know what "I love you" means?

Yes. During the last months of an Alzheimer's client, when her caregiver tells her "I love you" she responds by saying "I love you too"

How can I treat a stomach that twitches?

Calm your stomach by eating protein rich foods such as eggs, goat's milk, other healthy veggie-high protein dish and warm ginger tea (boil ginger in water).

What are the arguments for and against vaccines?

There are small quantities of harmful chemicals included in the vaccine. It is best to be given to toddler and not an infant and to a healthy senior and not a sick older adult.

Does stress on the heart in youth affect Alzheimer's pathology?

Sugar is one of the top causes in the disease progression of Alzheimers. Stress is second. Parasites and bad microbes are the third. Always oxygenate your body cells with exercise, whole foods, de-stress, avoidance of toxins such as sugar/drugs/meds and sleep.

Is it bad for your health if your heart starts beating fast?

You will feel dizzy. Sit and elevate legs. Calm yourself. I experienced this fast heart beat or tachycardia (after I ate a toxic food or substance or is stressed out). Cough and do deep breathing since our goal is to provide oxygenation to all cells. One doctor captured this fast heart beat in ECG but I opted for no surgery and meds. His explanation is that there is extra wiring in the heart. I took magnesium and calcium and Vit C and B to nourish my heart. Breath through your nose, whole foods and light exercise helps.

How does your body digest hard food?

Does your stomach acid soften it or does it simply remain inside your stomach? Digestive enzymes in the body (saliva by chewing, stomach) and from papaya and pineapple or in capsule form help in digestion. Not drinking too much when eating meat.

What types of substances does papain help digest?

Proteolytic enzymes help break proteins down into smaller protein fragments called peptides and amino acids. The mechanism by which papain breaks peptide bonds involves the use of a catalytic triad with a deprotonated cysteine which forms a covalent acyl-enzyme intermediate and frees the amino terminus of the peptide. In immunology, papain is known to cleave the Fc (crystallisable) portion of immunoglobulins (antibodies) from the Fab (antigen-binding) portion. Papain is a moderately heat-safe enzyme, with an equal temperature scope of 60 and 70 °C.

How long does it take regularly for the stomach to empty absolutely after a good meal. Is it a good eating habit not to eat during this time?

It takes 4 hrs to process meat and 30 min to process eggs. Constipation happens frequently in over medicine grown-ups. Pineapple and papaya have strong digestive enzymes important for digestion. Eat whole foods, move and exercise regularly and bite your food well.

When you drink coffee early morning before exercise, it is a stimulant helping your bowel movement in spite of the fact that it is maintained a strategic distance from by the individuals who needs to lose stomach fat.

What are some lesser known foods, drinks, and so forth that are useful for the digestive system or metabolism?

Mint family, ginger, peppermint and spearmint.

How can I prevent stomach acid in my sleep without needing medication?

Ultimately, the answer to heartburn and acid indigestion is to restore your natural gastric balance and function. Eating large amounts of processed foods and sugars is a surefire way to exacerbate acid reflux as it will upset the bacterial balance in your stomach and intestine.

Instead, you'll want to eat a lot of vegetables and other high-quality, ideally organic, unprocessed foods. Also, eliminate food triggers from your diet. Common culprits here include caffeine, alcohol, and nicotine products.

Next, you need to make sure you're getting enough beneficial bacteria from your diet with whole foods (garlic, apple cider vinegar, yogurt, pineapple, papaya, greens). This will help balance your bowel flora, which can help eliminate H. pylori bacteria naturally without resorting to antibiotics.

It will also aid in proper digestion and assimilation of your food. Ideally, you'll want to get your probiotics from fermented foods.

If you aren't eating fermented foods, you most likely need to supplement with a probiotic on a regular basis. Ideally, you'll want to include a variety of cultured foods and beverages in your diet, as each food will inoculate your gut with a variety of different microorganisms.

Fermented foods you can easily make at home include:

- Fermented vegetables
- Chutneys
- Cultured dairy, such as yoghurt, kefir, and sour cream
- Fish, such as mackerel

In Sympathetic Nervous System Why the digestion of food is slow? Where as in fight or flight we need more energy?

There are hormones involved in preparation (norepineprine), during and after (acetylcholine) the fight/flight reaction.

Preparation: The effect of norepinephrine on each target organ is to modify its state in a way that makes it more conducive to active body movement, often at a cost of increased energy use and increased wear and tear.

After the fight: The acetylcholine-mediated effects of the parasympathetic nervous system, which modifies most of the same organs into a state more conducive to rest, recovery, and digestion of food, and usually less costly in terms of energy expenditure.

I miss coffee. Is there a way to return to it?

Yes, heal your stomach, drink in the morning with soft boiled eggs, add boiled ginger and use decaf (freshly brewed), add tea, goat's milk and maple syrup or honey.

Is there any relationship between bipolar disorder and fast metabolism?

Yes, as most mental health issues are related to the microbiome (gut microbes) of the gut. Follow a healthy lifestyle to increase beneficial bacteria in the gut (from whole foods, with rest and relaxation to lessen stress, exercise, night time sleep) to improve mood and reduce anxiety (Butler MI, et al. Can J Psychiatry. 2019).

Microbes Help Produce Serotonin in Gut

Although serotonin is well known as a brain neurotransmitter, it is estimated that 90 percent of the body's serotonin is made in the digestive tract. In fact, altered levels of this peripheral serotonin have been linked to diseases such as irritable bowel syndrome, cardiovascular disease, and osteoporosis. Peripheral serotonin is produced in the digestive tract by enterochromaffin (EC) cells and also by particular types of immune cells and neurons.

Is it possible to change metabolism through diet?

Exercise, sleep, diet and mental disposition (less stress and anxiety) can help your metabolism. Do take probiotics and eat some pickled greens.

Which foods can speed up my metabolism?

Based on the lifestyle, age, sex and race, our body has nutritional needs Younger ones might need more healthy carbs and protein (rich in fiber) while older ones needs good fats and protein. When in disease state (mental health issues), our lipid metabolism is affected.

Despite the fact that unsaturated fats are the substrates richest in hydrogen for providing redox energy to the mitochondrial And so on, they are not used fundamentally as fuel in neural cells.

High vulnerability of brain tissue to oxidative stress is for the most part professed to be the basic reason. We eat whole foods to prevent inflammation.

Is a person's metabolic rate identified with aging?

Age is one of the most significant factors of changes in energy metabolism, important for physiological functions including nutrient absorption. The basal metabolic rate diminishes with age.

Skeletal musculature is a fundamental organ that expends the biggest piece of energy in the ordinary human body. The all out volume of skeletal muscle can be assessed by 24-hours creatinine discharge.

The volume of skeletal musculature decreases and the level of fat tissue increases with age.

It is demonstrated that the lessening in bulk with respect to add up to body might be completely in charge of the age-related decreases in basal metabolic rate. Energy consumption by physical action additionally decreases with atrophic changes of skeletal muscle.

Energy requirement in the older decreases. With reduction of energy admission, intake of basic nutrients decreases.

If energy intake, on the other hand, exceeds individual energy needs, fat amasses in the body. Muscle versus fat will in general collect in the stomach area in the older.

Fat tissue in the stomach cavity is associated directly with the liver through entry vein. Accumulation of stomach fat causes unsettling influence in glucose and lipid metabolism. It is demonstrated that glucose resistance diminishes with age.

Despite the fact that age contributes freely to the decay in glucose resistance, the decline in glucose tolerance might be halfway forestalled through changes of way of life factors.

We can delay the aging process of different physiological capacities by changing our dietary habits, halting smoking, exercise, and avoidance of parasites, toxins, molds and fungus.

What is the difference between a person with high metabolism and another one with low metabolism?

Low metabolism will have stronger side effects from medications while high metabolism have more side effects from medications, absorbs more nutrients, does not get drunk from alcohol easy, do not have allergies and have stronger immune system.

Do people with higher metabolism get sick more easily?

The way our bodies regulate and manage energy—our metabolism—and our body's ability to defend itself against pathogens—the immune response—are closely linked. Our body has electrical energies that are in sync. The highest in frequency are essential oils and lowest in frequency are canned foods. Sickness or disease are based on the energy, metabolism, liver health, immune system and all the cells in our body, working in harmony and fighting invading microbes such as parasites and virus.

Weight loss, loss of appetite and chronic health pain or health issues are caused by a fast metabolic rate and are symptoms of cancer.

Slow down your metabolism:

- Have a consistent meal time
- Get adequate sleep
- Add strength training
- Eating sufficient calories
- Stand and walk more, sit less
- Drink no alcohol and drink more water.
- Have less stress, get a massage and be with nature.
- Get adequate calcium (2:1 calcium: magnesium ratio with vitamin D)

What is the best natural remedy for diabetes 2?

Fig fruit is used as a laxative to relieve constipation. Fig LEAF is used for diabetes, high cholesterol, and skin conditions such as eczema, psoriasis, and vitiligo. Some people apply the milky sap (LATEX) from the tree directly to the skin to treat skin tumors and warts.

Bitter melon: These substances either work individually or together to help reduce blood sugar levels. It is also known that bitter melon contains a lectin that reduces blood glucose concentrations by acting on peripheral tissues and suppressing appetite, similar to the effects of insulin in the brain.

Fiber (steel oatmeal, physillium,veggies,beans) encapsulates fats and sugar out of the body.

Best remedy is to avoid sugar, sleep well, exercise, avoid toxins such as parasites, virus, molds, fungus, avoid smoking/too much alcohol. Do eat whole foods between 11am to 8pm.

What percentage of the US has type 2 diabetes?

About 30%

If you could hypothesize a possible way to cure diabetes what would you suggest?

Health education, exercise with a coach (30min to 1hr per day), nutrition with a coach (whole foods, fiber rich), genetic test and overall lifestyle change connecting with health conscious and like-minded people and community.

Do you know some good foods for people with low blood sugar? Is coffee good for them?

Here are 6 tips that give you their top recommendations to decrease cortisol levels and thus catabolic metabolism while you increase anabolic metabolism and experience optimal health.

Eliminate caffeine from your diet. It's the quickest way to reduce cortisol production and elevate the production of DHEA, the leading anabolic youth hormone. 200 mg of caffeine (one 12 oz mug of coffee) increases blood cortisol levels by 30% in one hour! Cortisol can remain elevated for up to 18 hours in the blood. This is the easiest step to decrease your catabolic metabolism and increase your anabolic metabolism.

Sleep deeper and longer. The average 50 year old has nighttime cortisol levels more than 30 times higher than the average 30 year old. Try taking melatonin, a natural hormone produced at night that helps regulate sleep/wake cycles, before going to sleep to boost your own melatonin production that also decreases with age.

Exercise regularly to build muscle mass and increase brain output of serotonin and dopamine, brain chemicals that reduce anxiety and depression.

Keep your blood sugar stable. Avoid sugar in the diet and refined carbohydrates to keep from spiking your insulin production. Eat frequent small meals balanced in protein, complex carbohydrates and good fats like olive oil and flaxseed oil. Diets rich in complex carbohydrates keep cortisol levels lower than low carbohydrate diets. Drink less caffeine rich drinks.

Keep well hydrated – dehydration puts the body in stress and raises cortisol levels. Keep pure water by your bed and drink it when you first wake up and before you go to sleep.

Take anti-stress supplements like B vitamins, minerals like calcium, magnesium, chromium and zinc, and antioxidants like vitamin C, alpha lipoic acid, grape seed extract, and Co Q 10. Adaptogen herbs like ginseng, astragalus, eleuthero, schizandra, Tulsi (holy basil) rhodiola and ashwagandha help the body cope with the side effects of stress and rebalance the metabolism. These supplement and herbs will not only lower cortisol levels but they will also help you decrease the effects of stress on the body by boosting the immune system.

Meditate or listen to relaxation music or sounds that promotes the production of alpha (focused alertness) and theta (relaxed) brain waves. Avoid jolting alarm clocks that take you from delta waves (deep sleep) to beta waves (agitated and anxious) and stimulants like caffeine that promote beta waves while suppressing alpha and theta waves.

If diabetes causes Alzheimer's disease, do all diabetics get Alzheimer's disease?

Yes. As we age, our body becomes rusty with many toxins such as sugar. Some people who died at 100 yrs of age have Alzheimer's in their brain but showed not very strong signs and symptoms.

Can yoga help to cure type 1 diabetes mellitus?

Insulin is needed. Some of the organs in our body did not release the insulin we need maybe because of toxins from sugar, fat, metals or inactivity. Each person is different. It is not too late to move, to exercise and do yoga.

There are scientists who are currently researching how to create a human pancreas.

Is low blood sugar genetic?

20:80 is my guess. Our genes affect us 20% of the time while our environment and lifestyle affects us 80% of the time (epigenetics).

Each person metabolize glucose or drugs or food in the liver differently. Pharmacogenetic tests classified these into 4 groups of people.

We have to choose good carbohydrates from whole foods (colored greens, fibrous whole foods) and avoid toxins (alcohol, soda, aspartame, processed foods, burned BBQ meat, etc). We sleep before 10pm and exercise 30min every day. We destress and be proactive with our own health.

In mammals the response to dietary glucose is more complex because it combines effects related to glucose metabolism itself and effects secondary to glucose-dependent hormonal modifications, mainly pancreatic stimulation of insulin secretion and inhibition of glucagon secretion. In the pancreatic β cells, glucose is the primary physiological stimulus for the regulation of insulin synthesis and secretion.

In the **liver, glucose, in the presence of insulin,** induces expression of genes encoding glucose transporters and glycolytic and lipogenic enzymes.

Although insulin and glucagon were long known as critical in regulating gene expression, it is only recently that carbohydrates also have been shown to play a key role in transcriptional regulation. DNA sequences and DNA binding complexes involved in the glucose-regulated gene expression have been characterized recently in liver and β cells.

For **glucose to act as a gene inducer, it must be metabolized.**

If you have diabetes, how can you prevent fainting?

Low glucose, lack of potassium and iron can cause fainting.

Potassium: sodium ratio is about 5:1 . Both can be found in whole foods, greens.

Iron-rich foods include molasses and dark chocolates. Nuts and small seeds have calcium,magnesium and iron.

Dehydration (by excess loss of water in urine in diabetics), hormonal fluctuations and lack of sleep can cause fainting. In seniors, it is more lack of potassium and in pregnant women, progesterone hormones widening the blood vessels.

How can I avoid developing diabetes?

We have to eat good fats and avoid soda, bad fats and other toxic sugar-rich processed foods. Start with clean alkaline water, fresh air, and avoidance of toxins (chemical cleaners, plastics,molds/fungus,fumes,metal toxins,other inflammatory substances/drugs/medications). Do liver detox once a month (citrus/pectin,other detoxifiers).

Get a massage once a week. Sleep during the night. Always have fiber, digestive enzymes and probiotic. Add seaweed and cooked/raw whole foods in your diet. Wash veggies with diluted vinegar water or salt water.

Do not eat moldy/left over foods. Always have a strong immune system by avoiding anxiety and chronic stress. Avoid caffeine, smoking (second hand smoke) and alcohol (too much).

What is the correlation between being in good shape and being free from cardiovascular diseases and diabetes?

No. There are skinny ones who have circulatory issues which is deeply rooted from nutrition (lack of Vitamin C and E to strengthen blood vessels, presence of air pollution and other toxins) and other unknowns.

- 55% of our health issues are attributed to environment (toxins, parasites, infections, etc) and behaviour (even during prenatals when inside the womb of our mothers)
- 5% genetics
- 20% health care

Why have endocrinological diseases like diabetes, thyroiditis, etc. become so common these days?

Stress is the answer with most of us not taking a nap and not getting uninterrupted 9 hours sleep.

Adrenals and liver come to the rescue as blood sugar levels drop. The endocrine pancreas, liver and adrenal glands work to normalize blood sugar and triglycerides.

Take care of your stress so it will be easier for you to prevent obesity, depression, sugar cravings and nerve pain which may start to happen at around 55 years of age. When we take care of our stress level, we take care of our metabolism, brain, whole body and we then prevent chronic diseases that lead to cancer.

Activities to make you happy

Beach stroll, dancing, watching comedians, laughing, sleeping at nigh, massage, happy and loving friends and relationships, spending time with family and friends, playing with your pets, gardening, singing, praying, deep breathing exercise, meditation.

Side effects of chronically elevated cortisol can include:

Anxiety, autoimmune diseases, cancer, chronic fatigue syndrome, common colds, hormone imbalance, irritable bowel disease, thyroid conditions, weight loss resistance. Cortisol is an indicator of severity of parasitic infections (Fleming MW. Comp Biochem Physiol B Biochem Mol Biol. 1997).

Needed nutrients

Digestive enzymes, vitamin C (citrus, kiwi, berries, tamarind), vitamin B, L-carnitine, chromium, anti-oxidants, fiber-rich foods (squash, yams, sulfur family of garlic and onions, greens, okra, radish), spearmint, ginger, beets, carrots, all root crops, sprouts, pineapple, papaya, taurine rich foods (breastmilk, sea algae, fish)

Adaptogenic herbs

- Eleuthero ginseng
- Holy basil
- Rodiola rosea
- ashwagandha
- Astralagus
- Sour date
- Mimosa pudica
  Extracts of Mimosa pudica are successful in wiping out harmful bacteria and can be useful in antibacterial products
- Medicinal mushrooms
  Mushrooms are rich in B vitamins such as riboflavin (B2), folate (B9), thiamine (B1), pantothenic acid (B5), and niacin (B3).
- Licorice root
- Valerian

Why could peripheral neuropathy worsen in a controlled diabetic patient?

Nerve pain and diabetes can be aggravated by lack of Vitamin B12 and B6 coupled with over medication. Take these energy Vitamin B complex during the day and calcium with magnesium during the night. Always eat whole foods (pineapple, fish, colored veggies). Vitamin B6 deficiency can decrease T cell population (J Immunol Res. 2017;2017:2197975. doi:10.1155/2017/2197975 Epub 2017 Mar 6).

In one seminar with chiropractors, they showed light therapy. As we age, we become deficient in these vitamins and decreasing acidity in our stomach (can be supplemented by Betaine HCL). See a nutritionist for digestive enzymes and probiotic in the evening or early morning 3hrs before or 3hrs after a meal to help with our metabolism. Fiber-rich foods raise blood sugar levels slowly which is important for people with insulin resistance (http://doi.org/10.1093/jn/nxx008).

How can I slow down my diabetes?

Kill the parasites that wrecks havoc in your organs: liver, kidneys, pancreas. They invade your liver and other organs, then the blood and the brain.

I am pre-diabetic, so this is what I did:

- kill parasites using tinctures from herbs, capsules, whole foods
- at night, eat apples and whole foods with healthy bacteria
- during lunch loaded with sulfur rich foods
- avoided unhealthy oils and sugar
- slept adequately at night
- went for body massage once a week
- walked barefoot on the beach
- avoided animal poops from dogs and cats
- boiled ginger, lemon, turmeric, cayenne, pepper and parsley as my warm tea
- mixed cooked bitter melon in my steel oatmeal

De-stress, adequate sleep, avoidance of toxins (drugs,alcohol,sugar, cigarettes, over medications) and taking whole foods rich in good fat (avocado, walnuts, fish) and fiber (encapsulates fats and sugar out of the body).

Add digestive enzymes (papaya, pineapple), prebiotic (raw garlic,raw carrots) and probiotic (pickled veggies) in your diet. Exercise at least 30min a day.

Can any info about blood conditions (pressure, sugar levels, etc.) be discerned by simply looking at properties of skin (i.e. sweat, oils, etc.)?

Yes. There are many. For breast cancer, any irregular skin growth, itchiness, redness and when you palpate with your two fingers, a tumorous growth. As the largest organ, the skin can show the health of our liver and other organs in our body. Excessive sweating, or hyperhidrosis, can be a warning sign of thyroid problems, diabetes or infection. Excessive sweating is also more common in people who are overweight or out of shape. Smell emanating from the skin also tells us of the health condition of the body. Pale color under the eyelid is a sign of lack of iron.

Blood clot symptoms in skin; Symptoms of superficial thrombophlebitis include:

- redness and inflammation of the skin along a vein.
- warmth of the skin and tissue around the vein.
- tenderness and pain that worsens with added pressure.
- pain in the limb.
- darkening of the skin over the vein.
- hardening of the vein.

Signs of liver damage

The liver is a hardy organ and carries much responsibility. It provides us with youthfulness and longevity when it operates effectively, and subjects us to premature aging and shortened life spans when it's not.

So how do you know if your liver is crying for help? Here are some visible physical signs:

- Puffiness between eyebrows
- Unable to tolerate cold in winter
- Feel feverish and find summer very uncomfortable
- Hemorrhoids
- Coated tongue
- Bad breath
- Excessive sweating

- Dark urine
- Small red 'spots' the size of a pinhead that come and go in various parts on the body
- Skin problems such as bruishing, eczema, acne, hives, itching, rashes. Skin may have dark pigmentation or spots on face, back of hands, forehead, or around the nose
- Jaundice (yellowing of skin)
- Eye problems (sensitivity to light, moving spots, double vision)
- Whites of eyes become yellow
- Loss of weight
- Obesity

Can I ever fully reverse diabetes after being so for 15 years?

Yes. Your determination to follow a healthy lifestyle in an important factor in your success to be healthy. The pituitary gland in the brain controls sex hormones, food cravings, sleep and stress. There is a relationship between gut health and mental health. Whole foods and fiber in them encapsulates fat and sugar out of the body. Exercise moves these toxins out of the body. Avoidance of toxins, sugar (sodas) and trans fat is one step. Add bitter melon and steel oat meal in daily meals. Kill parasites in the body. Avoid moldy foods. Sleep at night. Exercise in the sun. Type 2 Diabetes is a reversible condition using a low calorie diet (Newcastle University. 2017).

Will I get diabetes if I drink 1.5 liters of coke in an hour?

Yes, over time. The liver then turns the high amounts of sugar circulating our body into fat. Insulin and leptin act in the brain as adiposity negative feedback signals (Morton and Schwartz, 2011: Physiol. Rev. 91. 389.411 10.1152/physrev.00007.2010). The liver plays a major role in the modulation of the leptin signal and insulin resistance in obesity (PMID: 15788447 [Indexed for MEDLINE]). Within 40 minutes, the body has absorbed all of the caffeine from the Cola, causing a dilatation of pupils and an increase in blood pressure.

An hour after drinking the beverage, a sugar crash will begin, causing irritability and drowsiness.

Can eating boiled eggs with vinegar kept overnight really lower your sugar level or control diabetes?

Soft boiled eggs has sulfur which is cleansing to the body and so are yellow colored whole foods (including garlic, onions, yams with skin on). Vinegar helps in the absorption of many nutrients in whole foods.

Add probiotics, Vit C or lemon water in the mix. Exercise, sleep and de-stress count too.

Why I always have mouth infections?

I have experienced the same.

I love to eat moldy foods or just my lifestyle for inviting bugs of all sorts. Tea tree oil is antimicrobial, anti bacteria, antifungal and anti virus. I would make a gargle or mouthwash from it since in concentrated form of the essential oil it has burning sensation. I will also make a mouth wash every morn of sea salt and sage. You can also wash it with boiled water of guava leaves or comfrey.

From now on, I will be eating lots of fresh garlic chewing once a day and sulfur rich foods like the onion family, fresh aloe vera made into a juice with lemon water and maple syrup, avoiding so much refined sugar and processed foods including moldy foods and eat more pickled veggies (kimchi, kefir).

Aloe vera can increase the proliferation of lymphocytes and stimulate natural immunity through killer cell activity (parasitetesting.com).

See:

Vahedi, Ghasem & Taghavi, Mehdi & Maleki, Amin & Habibian, Reza. (2011). The effect of Aloe vera extract on humoral and cellular immune response in rabbit. African Journal of Biotechnology. 10.

Bacterial infections, which include ailments like bronchitis and pneumonia, are caused by single-celled organisms that can invade and thrive inside our bodies, reproducing on their own. Most bacterial infections can be treated with antibiotics that stop the colonies from growing larger.

Viral infections, such as the flu (influenza) and the common cold (rhinovirus), on the other hand, do not replicate on their own like bacteria does. Instead, viruses take over our cells and hijack them to get them pumping out more copies of the virus, so it spreads through our bodies like a hostile takeover.

Is there any medical proof of a connection between having cold showers on a daily basis, and being immune to the flu?

Any kind of acute cold exposure will stimulate the vagus nerve (part of the sensory somatic system) which controls gut inflammation. Cold showers stimulate your autonomic nervous system, improving stress reaction and relieves anxiety and fatigue.

There was a report in the news where children in Russia play in the snow (less clothing) after staying in a sauna and they are the ones who did not catch the cold.

Acute cold exposure increased total (36%), low (16%), and high frequency power (25%) and RMSSD (34%). A smaller increase in heart rate and blood pressure occurred at 10 degrees C during the handgrip test after cold acclimation. (Aviat Space Environ Med. 2008 Sep;79(9):875-82).

Note: When we help in showering seniors, we wet their feet first and using warm water as they are sensitive to cold. Our running water in California is treated with chlorine. So, we should not stay too long to not affect our lung function.

What are the most common age related diseases?

- Cancer, infections from parasites, bacteria and virus and organ damage.
- Eating less meat or methionine-rich foods slows aging.
- Sleeping at night helps us detox our cells from toxins.
- Parasites invade our cells and weakens our organs especially vulnerable during old age, and the end product is cancer (grows over time, at least for 20 years).
- Over exposure to air pollution and unclean water kills our lungs and hearts.

What is sepsis?

The most widely recognized source of infection bringing about sepsis are the lungs, abdomen, and the urinary tract. Normally, half of all sepsis cases begin as an infection in the lungs. No definitive source is found in 33% to one portion of cases.

Infections prompting sepsis are normally bacterial however can be parasitic or viral. While gram-negative bacteria were already the most well-known reason for sepsis, in the last decade gram-positive bacteria, most commonly staphylococci, are thought to cause over half of cases of sepsis.

How many eggs I should eat every day with some veggies and no carbs, in order to stay healthy?

1 soft boiled egg. Add exercise and colored veggies. De-stress and get adequate sleep and sleep before 10pm.

What to do or how to avoid getting a stomach ache after eating meat?

Include fiber rich whole foods with your dinner rich in meat, bite more, eat pineapple. 30min after or take digestive enzymes and before sleep time 1/4 tsp of apple juice vinegar in a glass of water.

How to control compulsive eating?

To calm your nerves, eat food rich in Vitamin B complex, yams, eggs and all sulfur- rich foods. To calm your nerves, eat food rich in Vitamin B complex, yams, eggs and all sulfur rich foods. Dr Daniel Amen in this book, Change your brain, change your life, wrote: Boost dopamine and serotonin with combo of green tea + 5HTP, learn how to distract yourself when you get a thought in your head more than 3x, structured goal setting, intense exercise, a balanced diet of whole foods, EPA/DHA omega-3, And I'm going to add probiotics in the list.

Note: Effects of supplementation with dietary green tea polyphenols on parasite resistance and acute phase protein response to *Haemonchus contortus* infection in lambs: An appropriate dose of dietary GTP supplementation can increase host resistance by reducing H. contortus burden and weight loss and suppressing blood APP expression (https://doi.org/10.1016/j.vetpar.2014.06.022).

- Follow the anti-parasitic diet in this site https://clubalthea.com/?s=parasites
- Exercise in early morning or late afternoon sunshine
- Add rosemary, ginger, onion and garlic in your diet, drinks and add ginger in your massage oil
- Add vitamin C rich foods and supplements
- Get weekly massage
- Dance and find your favorite relaxing music
- Surround yourself with positive people and environment

Is eating onion and yoghurt together bad for health?

Onion is rich in sulfur cleansing nutrients while yoghurt has probiotics, good bacteria. Yoghurt can lead to cancer if you consume it together with ham or meat. Several amounts of nitrates are usually added to prevent the meat decomposition and botulin to extend their lifespan.

Both of that food combination will turn into nitrosamine and carcinogenic when the organic nitrate acid met with artificial nitrate inside our body.

What happens if you eat raw taro?

Raw taro has oxalates that can harm your kidneys. Cooked taro has many health benefits because of its many nutrients from vitamins to minerals and anti-parasitic actions.

What are the healthy benefits of corn beef hash?

The bone marrow of the beef can help with your immune system and prevent infection. Make bone broth with tomatoes for Vit C.

Are genes the decisive operator in resilience to external factors?

Our nervous system, immune system, lifestyle and environment and genes are all decisive factors.

What food exacerbates inflammatory response if you are arthritic?

- Fried and processed. Fried and processed foods.
- AGEs. Lower your AGEs.
- Sugars and refined carbs. Sugars and refined carbs.
- Dairy. Dairy products.
- Alcohol and tobacco.
- Salt and preservatives.
- Corn oil

What explicit foods normally shed fat from your body?

Sour and bitter fruits and veggies. Tamarind, citrus and guava (vitamin C rich) and sulfur rich such asparagus, garlic, onions, mustard

Is there a particular food that is more healthy than any other?

Sour fruits and bitter greens, purslane leaves, dandelion leaves, kiwi and blueberries.

What healthy breakfast foods have negative health effects in the long term?

Coffee. For seniors with ulcers, diabetes, gastritis or osteoporosis, the effects of caffeine may be more harmful and not worth the risk. If you do drink a cup in the morning, make it a fresh batch and add ginger.

What diet would you need to attempt to try that you had more will power?

Bitter greens and sour fruits as they are both anti-cancer too.

How can drinking milk cause health issues?

Undigested fat from milk taxes the liver. Milk and other dairy products are the top source of saturated fat in the American diet, contributing to heart disease, type 2 diabetes, and Alzheimer's disease. Studies have also linked dairy to an increased risk of breast, ovarian, and prostate cancers.

What are the healthy foods for 50-year-old people?

If retired, cook and prepare your meals daily. If not retired, use simple foods and prepared with proper hygiene.

If one of the family members died of cancer, do a liver cleansing food to kill infections or parasites.

Aspire to eat your nutrients from foods and not be over medicated.

Bitter greens, bananas, soft boiled egg, lemons, soups, salads (washed with vinegar or salt water), sweet potatoes, root veggies and sour fruits. Avoid foods with trans fat, molds, additives, processed salt or sugar, alcohol, caffeine, restaurant foods and fast foods, soda, milk and cheese and red meat.

Morning foods: eggs, soy or almond milk, green tea or fresh ginger with lemon tea, soup, filtered water), boiled sweet potatoes or yams, berries

Late afternoon and lunch foods: apples, bananas, avocado, soup, calcium and magnesium rich foods, coconut water.

Is eating between meals worse than having meals that respect a precise time of the day that are too large?

Calorie restriction helps us live longer and can be used to treat cancer. I believe it is still healthy to have one small healthy meal. But as we age (over 65yrs of age), we need to eat small meals every 3hrs or so. Boiled fresh ginger with lemon helps in cleansing our cells.

Does sugar prolong illness?

Sugar is food for cancer cells, it shrinks our brain, shortens our lifespan, damages our cells and prevents the absorption of important nutrients. A sugar-laden diet may raise your risk of dying of heart disease even if you aren't overweight.

Eat less. Eat rice soup with ginger.

Read more: https://www.newscientist.com/article/2105986-what-you-eat-when-youre-sick-may-determine-if-youll-get-better/#ixzz5zin2gTHL

Read more: https://www.newscientist.com/article/2105986-what-you-eat-when-youre-sick-may-determine-if-youll-get-better/#ixzz5zin2gTHL

What sort of foods and vitamins can keep your nervous system healthy?

Good fats, omega 3 rich foods, sulfur rich foods, phosphorous, potassium,Vitamin B complex, probiotics, digestive enzymes and all whole foods.

When do we have to eat salad/veggies, directly before dinner or thirty minutes before?

Try a short 15min or more exercise before your meal.

I will start with warm soup and then eat salad (which must be washed with diluted vinegar or salt water and cook your greens well especially the **cabbage family to prevent bloating**). Eat your meals during the day and not late at night. I eat one fresh apple (not over ripe) in the evening as it contains 100 million good bacteria. Do not eat raw (over ripe) banana before bedtime and many other foods are not eaten an hour before bedtime, except for celery juice and hormone free milk with chocolate powder. We need to sleep before 10am and eat the next morning at 10am to allow for short fasting for those who want to detox.

How effective is " the diet of dark chocolate and black coffee"?

Not successful. You get magnesium in many foods aside from dark chocolates. And it is in the ratio of 40:60, 40% magnesium and 60% calcium with Vit C and D and zinc to be absorbed. Coffee is a strong stimulant and acidic to be taken in limited amount in the morning before exercise. You can mix half fresh ginger tea and half coffee sweetened with honey or maple syrup. You may add ginger to the coffee in the morning.

Green tea is preferred for all, not black coffee or black tea. Some people with brain cancer uses a low calorie ketogenic diet of high good fat, and a little carbs and protein. Sleep will help you lose weight, including 15-minute exercise a day, deep breathing and a happy disposition.

How would you know whether a food has a specific effect?

My mother swears by eating persimmons (yellow colored fruit rich in Vitamin A) that her eye itchiness goes away within an hour. We have a good bowel movement with good healthy food and stomach ache/loose bowel or constipation with bad food. We sleep better and if not, we lack probiotics or digestive enzymes to balance the bacteria in our gut.

What foods should an individual avoid eating to lose 1-2 lb a week?

Sugar, soda and juices, over ripe fruits, rice and bread, processed meat, cheese and dairy and not sleeping well.

Avoid high protein diet as they boost artery-clogging plaque. Arginine and Leucine amino acids in meat in high quantity can clog arteries (Washington University School of Medicine 2020).

Does adding benefiber to milk work?

It is rich in pysillium husk and is sweet. Depending on the age of the child or for seniors with constipation, other foods (fruits) can facilitate bowel movement like prunes and other fruits.

How much salad should you eat per meal?

Lunch: Eat high fat (nuts,meat) during the day 1 cup of raw greens/ lettuce. A standard serve of vegetables is 75 grams or: ½ cup cooked greens (spinach) or orange vegetables (for example, broccoli, spinach, carrots or pumpkin); ½ cup cooked dried or canned beans, peas or lentils Dinner: Eat 2-4hrs before bedtime, protein rich (less fat). Your food consumption every day relies upon your health goals, issues, stress, way of life, genetics and different factors. When your body tells you that you are full, then you can stop. But meds interfere with our satiety. Flavor and aroma will assist us with our craving.

As we age, we absorb less of the nutrients that we need. Our gut flora must be healthy to absorb all the nutrients from foods/supplements.

Let us take for an example of some drugs or meds that we take. Let us say we are taking TUMS, the un-absorbed calcium in it (free calcium) blocks the absorption of food-based calcium. Calcium citrate is still well absorbed even without food and may be better absorbed by older adults that have less digestive enzymes. The RDA for calcium is 1000 mg and increases with age. TUMs is an over-the-counter antacid with calcium carbonate. It is primarily excreted through the colon (75%) as unabsorbed calcium. Do take calcium and magnesium at 60:40 ratio.

Another example is iron that cancels calcium absorption and vice versa. So we eat iron rich food in the morning and calcium rich foods in the evening/afternoon. Or take our iron liquid supplement (Fluradix) in the morning and calcium/magnesium/Vit D/C in the evening.

And that most chemical process in the body is facilitated by the presence of Vitamin C and some enzymes.

Will viruses and different pathogens cause lower levels of nutrients in the body?

Yes, the parasite share in the nutrients that you ingest. A human host is a nutrient-rich, warm, and moist environment, which remains at a uniform temperature and constantly renews itself. It is not surprising that many microorganisms have evolved the ability to survive and reproduce in this desirable niche.

What are the good foods for people with low blood sugar? Is coffee good for them?

Here are ways to help decrease cortisol levels and catabolic metabolism while you increase anabolic metabolism and experience ideal health.

Reduce caffeine intake to morning only or avoid them.
It's the fastest method to lessen cortisol production and elevate the production of DHEA, the main anabolic youth hormone. The body manufactures DHEA naturally in the adrenal glands. *Adrenal* glands produce hormones that help regulate your metabolism, immune system, blood pressure, response to *stress* and other essential functions.

Sleep deeper and longer.

- Exercise regularly to build muscle and increase brain output of serotonin and dopamine, brain chemicals that decrease depression and anxiety.
- Keep your blood sugar stable. Avoid sugar in the eating regimen and refined carbohydrates to keep from spiking your insulin production.
- Eat frequent small meals balanced in soluble fiber-rich foods, protein, complex carbohydrates and good fats like fish oil, olive oil and flaxseed oil.

  Note: Eat less insoluble fiber in skin of fruits and veggies (worms multiply easy). (https://pdfs.semanticscholar.org/f6d2/d2d560d2d727d5d39232ab0b85ad380db24f.pdf).
  Oat hull fiber is an ingredient made by grinding and purifying the outermost protective layer of the oat grain. It consists mainly of lignin, cellulose and hemicellulose and, thus, is considered a rich source of insoluble dietary fiber (up to 90%).

- Take anti-stress supplements like B vitamins, minerals like calcium, magnesium, chromium and zinc, and antioxidants like nutrient vitamin C, alpha lipoic, grape seed concentrate, and CoQ10 (must be taken with STATINS meds). These supplements and herbs won't just lower cortisol levels however they will also enable you to decrease the effects of stress on the body by boosting the immune system.
- **Meditate or listen to relaxation tapes to promote the production of alpha (focused alertness) and theta (relaxed) brain waves.**

For what reason does all the body fat go to the body?

Lack of CLA, good fat from fish oil, lack of sleep, lack of Vitamin C, Omega 3 and D, hormonal imbalance. Your body must dispose of fat deposits through a series of complicated metabolic pathways. The byproducts of fat metabolism leave your body: As water, through your skin (when you sweat) and your kidneys (when you urinate). As carbon dioxide, through your lungs (when you breathe out).

How would you treat early morning acid in the stomach?

Drink water with baking soda, add a little molasses or maple syrup. Deep breathing and light exercise (squatting with deep breathing). When stomach acid moves up the esophagus, it can irritate the vocal cords.

This is often worse in the morning, after lying down all night and may subside during the day. Eat more veggies which are alkaline and protein rich breakfast.

How does your body digest hard food? How would you treat early morning acid in the stomach?

Digestive enzymes from papaya and pineapple or in capsule form. Saliva - by chewing a little longer. Not drinking too much when eating meat, drinking more 30 minutes before and after eating to not dilute stomach acids.

Why is my stomach sensitive to alcohol?

Alcohol is acidic, damaging tissues and impedes gastric enzymes. Do eat protein rich food when drinking alcohol and choose one with lower strength. For beers, choose local and not pasteurize for the beneficial effects of enzymes and hops. Breastfeeding provides protection to the stomach lining until adulthood. Blame parasites. Why are millions of people allergic to peanuts or pollen, but hardly anyone seems to have a reaction to rice or raisins? Because only some of these things carry molecules similar to those found in parasites that send our immune systems into hyperdrive, according to a new study (doi:10.1126/science.aad4791). Researchers were surprised when they found that intestinal worms, so-called Helminths (Toxocara Canis) from animals, actually have an influence on allergy- and asthma risk in humans (University of Bergen 2017).

What is the difference between men and women in metabolising alcohol?

How often women tend to drink and what happens to their bodies when they do is different when compared to men.

- ✓ Self-report surveys of men and women in the United States show that alcohol use is more prevalent among men than women.
- ✓ Men are more likely than women to become alcohol dependent.
- ✓ Binge drinking (such as consumption of five or more drinks per occasion on 5 or more days in the past month) is most common among women ages 18 to 25.
- ✓ Among racial groups, women's drinking is more prevalent among whites, although black women are more likely to drink heavily.
- ✓ Women absorb and metabolize alcohol differently than men.
- ✓ Women generally have less body water than men of similar body weight, so that women achieve higher concentrations of alcohol in the blood after drinking equivalent amounts of alcohol.
- ✓ Women DO appear to eliminate alcohol from the blood faster than men. This finding may be explained by women's higher liver volume per unit lean body mass, because alcohol is metabolized almost entirely in the liver.

Hormonal Factors, Part 2

- • WOMEN: Alcohol increases estrogen levels. Birth control pills or other medicine with estrogen increase intoxication.
  MEN: Alcohol also increases estrogen levels in men. Chronic alcoholism has been associated with loss of body hair and muscle mass, development of swollen breasts and shrunken testicles, and impotence.
  Source: NIAAA
  Source: www.factsontap.org

This section is about childbirth, nutrition,
and care for infants and mothers.

A POEM FOR MY GRANDMA

(http://www.clubalthea.com) from an ebook written by Connie Dello Buono, Birthing Ways Healing Ways 408-854-1883 motherhealth@ gmail.com

Grandmother

At 95 years of age, she now lays her tired hardworking body on the bed. Her six living children have just visited her to comfort her aging body. I called my mother and asked how grandma was doing since I'm more than 12,000 miles away from home. She said that she sometimes shows moments of strength whenever she is cared for by her family. Her family has grown to more than 36 grandchildren and 20 great grandchildren.

Blessed be my grandmother for she has endured the test of time. Many years ago she would blow air on my head and utter prayers and blessings before I had to go to another island. I remember now why I value the old and hand made things in life.

I can still see her sewing a quilt by hand from remnants of clothes she had asked for from the neighbor's shop. She would smile and proudly present to me her only hand-made quilt blanket and tell me that she will make pillow cases for my family. We did use her pillows and pillow cases for a long time.

Blessed be my grandmother who takes care of the old and used and made them into valuable items. She would sleep with me and give me a massage whenever I had a fever. That may be the reason why I don't have to take medications when I have a fever now. She wets me with warm compresses all over my body and massaged me with coconut oil. For different kinds of ailments she would use boiled herbs, chewed plants, incense, chants and prayers. For hours she would stir coconut juice into oil in a hot burning wooden stove.

Her strongest potion was her loving hands that would knead and roll my body and heal me like no other. Like a salesperson for many afternoons she would bring breads and snacks to the farmers in the fields. Blessed be my grandmother who heals and makes every time an important value never to be lost.

Her laboring hands and feet are strong, short and old. She was an apprentice midwife whenever any one of her daughters and daughters-in-law were having a baby. With her strong and commanding voice, she would coach them to bear down and push their babies. She was there to wash them and their babies after birth. Her healing hands provided infant massage and postpartum bliss for a new mother. She was their teacher in the first few years of mothering. Blessed be my grandmother who values herself as a woman and mother.

She would tell us stories of her adventures during World War II. Every day her family had to move to another hiding place away from the Japanese. She would be carrying two pots full of cooked yams or rice and chicken adobo. She would also feed the evacuating friends and family from the city. She made sure that she comforted her children every minute of the day. It took 40 years before her younger son left her to marry. But even then, her younger son would always see her everyday and give her bread and snacks. Blessed be my grandmother for her caring ways.

Every time there was someone who needed to be prayed for, she is summoned. She prayed and chanted in Latin and Visayan. She led the prayer meetings. She taught us her grandchildren how to respond and pray with her while we giggled at the foreign words. She never spanked us her grandchildren but her voice propels us to follow her just like our mothers. Maybe she was the other mother who mothered us when our mothers were busy. She was there when we are young and helpless. Blessed be my grandmother who taught us how to kneel and pray and sing vespers.

When everyone in the family is afraid she shows her strength and courage. When friends are mourning she prays with them and when one is sick she lays hand on her/him. When one is in crisis like quarreling husband and wife, she is the mediator. She made sure that we respect the old people. She made sure that we have said our prayers. Blessed be my grandmother Claudia Defensor Poral for she taught me how to cry, be strong, be a woman and now be a mother.

ABCs

You may call this section - the A to Z topics and thoughts for pregnant mothers. If you think of other topics that you want included, please let me know (connie@motherhealth.com). Some of the sources here are from my own personal experience as a homebirth mother and childbirth educator.

Acidophilus

Acidophilus may aid digestion and absorption of food nutrients and produce B-complex vitamins and vitamin K. It inhibits growth of other organisms by competing for nutrients, altering the pH environment, or producing bacteriocins, such as hydrogen peroxide, lactic acid, or acetic acid. Available in various dosages, in cultures ranging from 500 million to 4 billion viable organisms of L. acidophilus, in capsules, granules, powders, softgels, suppositories, tablets, milk and yogurts.

Acidophilus maybe useful as an aid in the treatment and prevention of bacterial vaginosis and vaginal yeast infections due to Candida Albicans. It may exert antibacterial activity against Helicobacter pylori or other intestinal bacteria. Human studies have demonstrated that the ingestion of L. acidophilus reduces the concentration of certain fecal enzymes that promote the formation of carcinogens in the colon.

Eat a healthy amount of yogurt when pregnant. Babies over 9 months old can also benefit from eating yogurt. Mothers with group B strep and other related infections do well with the capsule form plus vitamin C and Echinacea herb. A cup of yogurt a day drives the unwanted organisms away. Some mothers who took Acidophilus (in capsule form), vitamin C with bioflavinoids (regular dose) and echinacea (an immune booster herb) in tincture form have reduced their Group B Strep infection to what their body can fight, strengthened the amniotic sac and other beneficial results.

Ayurveda

Some mothers (especially from India) who practices the principles of Ayurveda balance their food with the body's physiology and personality.

Anesthesia (Epidural)

In animals edipural anesthesia has interfered with maternal attachment and the onset of mothering behavior by blocking the sensory stimuli for the central release of oxytoxin.

Anxiety

High-anxiety states affect the laboring mother. It can affect oxygenation and the flow of nutrients to the fetus and it has been correlated with abnormal decreases in fetal movement. It has also been associated with uterine dysfunction in labor and other debilitating labor patterns.

Anxiety

can be transformed by a mother with a strong will, focus and concentration, knowledge of what is happening and faith in herself. The flow of oxytocin during labor can be sustained and the ejectory reflex remain largely unimpeded.

Blue Cohosh

Blue cohosh is an agent to induce labor. It contains glycoside which stimulates smooth muscle in the uterus. It is not to be used in clients with heart disease.

Breech presentation

The baby's buttocks or legs, and not his head, are positioned against the cervix during labor.

Birth control

Birth control using the combination of mucus method, rhythm, and abstinence can be beneficial to most mothers. When the menstruation comes at day one, start counting and on day 10 till day 17 abstain from sex. Check the mucus between day 10 till day 16. The stretchy egg-white mucus is indicative of the ovulation period. Use condoms, diaphragm or abstinence during the fertile days.

Breastfeeding

Breastfeeding is likened to the child's connection with the umbilical cord when inside the womb. Keys in succeeding in breastfeeding include an unmedicated birth, early sucking, and making sure that the baby sucks the breast comfortably.

Some mothers are fortunate to get support from those who have experienced breastfeeding their babies. Seeking help from other moms, reading books on breastfeeding, joining support groups and using mothering instincts can all help. But without a full commitment to breastfeed her baby, a mother might be tempted not to breastfeed.

Knowing that breastmilk contains sleep inducing chemicals and that breastmilk is best nutrition for the baby might change the minds of some mothers. Challenges such as breast engorgement and sore nipples can be prevented when baby is fed on demand and comfortably. Mom should be as well rested as possible and eating healthy foods. The ease and convenience that breastfeeding affords the baby and moms are some of the surprising rewards.

Bottle-feeding

Consuming alternate food sources or using pumped breastmilk stored properly can help working mothers (see pumping breastmilk before returning to work).

Caesarean Operations

Caesarean operation is the delivery of the fetus through the abdominal and uterine walls after the twenty-eight week of pregnancy. In about 1%

of the total number of deliveries these operations are medically necessary. It is increasingly being performed under epidural rather than general anesthetic. This removes the risks associated with general anaesthetic and enables the mother to see and hold her baby at birth. Of the caesarean operations discussed in the published Report on Confidential Enquiries into Maternal Deaths in England and Wales 1979-1981 (DHSS, 1986), 70% were performed for hypertensive disease of pregnancy, fetal distress, or failure or delay of progress in labor.

Midwives and doulas show mothers how to cope during labor and how to summon their mothering wisdom and power. Many Caesarean operations can be prevented when mother is with a midwife and or a doula. Calm, healthy and full term babies are those born vaginally and breastfed a few minutes after birth. Some mothers feel that breastfeeding is affected by Caesarean operations. In unmedicated and natural birth, recovery is much faster for the mom and baby is not depressed.

One mother who had been drinking gallons of milk heavily during her first pregnancy had a Caesarean operation. For her second pregnancy, she was under the care of a midwife. She did not drink gallons of milk and she had a home birth for her second baby. Another mother that I personally helped during her labor had a Caesarean operation due to arrest in dilatation according to her doctors. She was starved for 20 hours and laying on her back she asked for more epidurals, one after another. Sometimes breastfeeding can't happen right away because of mom's exhaustion and pain after surgery.

Colic

The term "colic" describes a frequent symptom complex of paroxysmal abdominal pain, presumably of intestinal origin, and of severe crying. It occurs usually in infants younger than three months of age. Massage and seeing a chiropractor can help the infant.

Contraception

There are many natural ways of preventing conception: diaphragm or contraceptive cap, condom, abstinence, Rhythm method and the Mucus

Billing Method. The Mucus Billing Method uses the presence of the stretchy and sticky mucus to signal fertility periods which occurs at the 14th day from the start of menstruation. Coupled with checking body temperature which would rise by about one degree when taken early in the morning and noting the first day of menstruation in a calendar and counting day 10 to day 17 as the fertile week, this natural method has proven successfull in most women. Abstinence and or the use of condom or diaphragm should be used during the fertile days.

Diapers

Washing cloth diapers during the first year helps save money, makes a cleaner earth and keeps your baby's skin away from whatever toxins there may be in the disposable diapers.

Dystocia

Failure to progress has been a major cause of the rise in cesareans in the United States. After 45 hours of labor, the doctor advises the mother of the need for a cesarean operation. Dystocia is caused by a combination of the following factors: weak contractions, a greater-than-average size baby or a relatively small bony pelvis. Upright position and getting doulas and midwives can help prevent unnecessary c-sections.

Eating foods rich in iron and Vitamin C (with bioflavinoids strengthens the amniotic bag and prevents infection) and Vitamin K (rich in alfalfa sprouts) which helps prevents blood clotting. Cooking in cast iron pots or pans, and using other herbal remedies such as yellow dock root can help prevent anemia. As the last resort when supplementation is necessary, taking chelated iron supplements can also help.

Echinacea drops can help strengthen the immune system and fight other minor infections. One drop for every half a pound of body weight per dose. Extract of echinacea stimulates phagocytosis and increases respiratory cellular activity and mobility of leukocytes. In vitro studies using the fresh-pressed juice of the aerial portion of echinacea and the aqueous extract of the roots inhibited influenza, herpes infections, and vesicular stomatitis virus. In vitro studies indicate that the polyphenols from echinacea protect collagen against free radical attack.

Emergency Childbirth.

Epidural Analgesia

Epidural analgesia is the introduction of a local anesthetic into the epidural space. Continuous epidural analgesia gives 80-90% of mothers complete pain relief in labor. Approximately 3% of the epidurals are completely ineffective. Some of the possible complications of epidural include: maternal hypotension, puncture of the dura mater causing leakage of the cerebrospinal fluid, toxic reaction to local anaesthetic, retention of urine, infection, fetal bradycardia/slow heartbeat (fetal distress), respiratory arrest, and sense of deprivation.

Epidural or analgesia of any form during labor can be unnecessary if the mom has a midwife and doula and she listens to her body. She must ready her body for the work that labor entails. She should use various means of relieving pain: upright position, counterpressure, listening to the pushing urges of the body, hot compresses, warm shower. She must prepare her energetic and well nourished body through proper nutrition and exercises. The foremost factor about the impending pain during labor is awareness that the body is designed to labor naturally and that fear prolongs labor and makes it more painful.

Episiotomy

An episiotomy is an incision through the perineum and perineal body. The perineal body is a pyramid of muscle and fibrous tissue situated between the vagina and the rectum. A mother who trusts in her body, listens to it and has a healthy lifestyle with good nutrition and labors at home before going to the hospital can be spared the episiotomy, a cut that takes longer to heal and hurts more than having a baby.

Father

When you and your partner work together from the moment of conception till the baby is growing and needing both your time, your mothering is easy and your marriage grows stronger. The father will also feel that joyful sacrifice that you feel. He will then understand why you behave in such ways and how to be there at the right time for you and your baby. Fathers are also like expectant mothers, anxious of their new role as fathers. They are now serious in making more money for the new addition to the family. They view themselves as provider and giver of financial and emotional stability.

As everyone thinks of the mother's needs, the father is left on his own emotional needs. He senses the need to share in owning the birth of the baby and to take part in the unfolding of this new life.

He needs the reassurance that everything will work well. We should accept the many roles of our partner as provider, birth assistant, massage therapist and health care giver at home.

Go get a hot compress, call my labor support, midwife or doctor and shut your mouth, hubby. Listen to a laboring woman, don't disturb or talk to her when she is feeling the discomfort from the stretching of her bottom brought about by the descending baby. A hot compress (wet cloth) when applied to the opening yoni provides relief during labor.

Help me

Ask your friends to bring a meal for you after the baby is born. Many will be happy to accomodate your need for meals for the first few days. Help me do some household chores, hubby.

Honey

Honey can cause infant botulism, a serious disease for babies. It affects the babies nerves and muscles causing acute, flaccid paralytic illness caused by a neurotoxin. A baby who has this disease may be weak, constipated and eat poorly. Honey is safe for babbies over one year old. Foodborne botulism is best prevented by adhering to safe methods of home canning (pressure cooker and acidification), by avoiding suspicious foods, and by heating all home-canned foods for 80°C for at least 5 min.

Breastfeeding appears to slow the onset of infant botulism and to diminish the risk of respiratory arrest in infants in whom the disease develop. Feed only breastmilk for the first nine months.

I love you

Say I love you baby as soon as the baby is born.

Just push the baby out

Push when your body tells you to push.

Kind words

Let's spread these kind words of comfort for all laboring mothers: your laboring well for your baby, your body is doing what it supposed to do during birth and you are a woman, capable of birthing life and full of body wisdom.

Labor

Labor is real work for most first time moms. Fear prolongs labor. Standing in the shower, semi-squatting or sitting in the toilet, side lying, shaking the belly (belly dancing) and singing hastens the birth with less discomforts.

Life should be celebrated, call a Midwife (California Association of Midwives - 800-829-5791; American College of Nurse Midwives - 202-289-0171; Midwives Alliance of North America - 615-764-5561).

Midwives

Midwives are keepers of the normal birth. My midwife kept my pregnancy normal with low risks. The personal touch of care and service from my midwife from the prenatal visits to the postpartum care made my mothering role rewarding and fulfilling.

Mother

Easing the baby's transition from the womb to the outside world is the most important task of the mother. The mother who is conscious of the need of the child who is used to the life inside her womb bonds well with the baby. She knows and feels the baby's needs to breastfeed, sleep and be cared for by her loving hands and presence. A happy mom breeds a happy baby. A healthy diet makes a healthy mother and baby.

The smile of the baby is the sign of a contented baby and the sign of a nurturing mother. A healthy baby who seldom cries is a result of the non- stop care of the mother who feeds, cleans, and provide the comforts of her baby. The presence of the mother comforts the baby and the presence of the father or other family members are an extra bonus. That extra leap of growth from the bonding with the parents makes baby feel loved and secure.

Newborns

Newborns, nurture them for they will only be infants for a short time.
Open your body
Open up and embrace your baby at every contraction.

Place of Birth

The mother should be present in the birth process. She listens to the sensations of her body. She should feel comfortable and relaxed. Her determination to ease the baby's transition from the womb to the outside world would mean more energy to birth the baby. Her goal during birthing is for less trauma for the baby when inside and outside the womb.

She should choose the people and place that give the most comfort to her. Some mothers deliver their babies in the comfort of their home while others deliver their babies with little or no medication in the hospital. They know that the child within should be born as naturally as possible. Once the child is born, external forces in its surroundings have an impact on the success of its growth and health. The calmer the birth and delivery, the calmer the baby. The longer the baby stays in a healthy womb, the healthier the baby when born.

Quiet please

Laboring mother inside, quiet please.
Return control to the mother
Listen to the mothers before us, they have labored and endured it all without drugs.

Sleep

When putting the baby to sleep, the natural way to mother is:
To use the healing power of touch or massage.
To make skin to skin contact and to let the baby feels your heartbeat.
To make sure that the baby is clothed and positioned comfortably.
Sleeping with the baby during the early months of life outside the womb attunes mom to the baby's needs. Newborns need to be fed and changed constantly. They sleep well when the mom attends to baby's needs at every moment.

They feel the sense of security in the arms of their moms and listen to the soothing voice with admiration. A comforting bliss for both mom and baby follows. Some moms are surprised that they don't even have to rock or burp the baby who sleeps on her/his side after breastfeeding. Seeing the face of the mom before a nap helps many babies fall asleep and they go to sleep again when touched by the mother.

Taking

Heed the advice of mothers before us to endure the strain of caring for our babies. When exhaustion is forthcoming, mom should take a rest. Also it is a good idea to sleep when the baby sleeps.

Understand birth without fear

Why the fuss or fear? You are a woman and you are designed to birth a baby by listening to your body's wisdom. Get a midwife or a doula to comfort you during labor and birth.

Vow not to harm the newborn

To circumcise or not is not our business but the person who has the foreskin. Let's not count the numbers of sensory nerves attached to their skin that might be severed during the process of circumcision. If we do circumcise for religious reasons, it is a good idea to wait after a week when the clotting mechanism of the newborn is already intact. 13% of pediatricians surveyed did not know that the foreskin protects the glans, provides tissue for natural erection, defends against bacteria ad viruses, lubricates and has fine touch receptivity and full range of sexual response. 22% did not know that the proper care of a young child's foreskin is simply wash the external genitalia.

Womb

A pregnant mother who talks to her baby, touches her belly with soothing massage and thinks of her baby while eating healthy foods, fares well during labor and delivery. Bonding starts from the womb while the mother is conscious of the growing life inside her. The mother understands that the baby experiences much of the same feeling she has.

Yeast infection

Some pregnant mothers who have a cheesy discharge from their yoni do well with washing their yonies with few drops of Tea Tree oil (has antibacterial and antifungal properties) or diluted water with vinegar or some dash of herbs like golden seal, sage and comfrey.

REFERENCES

BehrMan, Kliegman, Arvin. Nelson Textbook of Pediatrics,W.B Saunders Company, 1996

Fetrow C, Avila J. Professional's Handbook of Complimentary & Alternative Medicines. Springhouse, 1999.

Sears W, Sears M. The Baby Book, Little, Brown and Company,1993

Circumcision Web Site References and Further Reading:

A list of pertinent websites can be found at: http://www.nocirc.org

A.M.E. (Association contre la Mutilacion des Enfants): http://www.enfant. org email: ame@enfant.org

Billy R., Circumcision Exposed: Rethinking a Medical and Cultural Tradition, The Crossing Press, POB 1048 Freedom California 95018

In Memory of the Sexually Mutilated Child: http://www. sexuallymutilatedchild.org

NORM (National Organization of Restoring Men): http://www.norm.org

ANEMIA

When to supplement with iron

Anemia is defined as a hematocrit <30, and Hemoglobin <10g. These indicators reflect the oxygenation of the tissues of the mother and therefore the babies. This varies with practitioners, however. Before the hemoglobin (Hgb) in the blood dips down to 10.5 grams and hematocrit value of less than 32% (Hct), pregnant moms should take iron supplements (40 mg chelated capsule form, 3x a day) in order not to be risked out from natural unmedicated birth in the hospital or homebirth. If a homebirth mom is not eating at least five servings of colorful fruits and vegetables a day, prenatal multivitamin and mineral supplement are recommended. Moms who have heavy menstrual periods, have been taking pills before conception and had history of low iron levels should take iron supplements. Iron supplements are best absorbed in chelated form and in combination with folic, vitamin C and B12. Medications taken before or during pregnancy can interfere with the way our body absorbs, utilizes, and excretes micronutrients. For example, antibiotics can hinder the availability of some B vitamins, vitamin C, potassium and calcium. And because they can destroy bacteria in the intestines, antibiotics also interfere with the synthesis of vitamin K, an important vitamin that helps in blood clotting.

Hormone-containing drugs like birth control pills appear to lower levels of some vitamins, including vitamin B6, folic acid and vitamin C. Caffeine containing foods such as coffee inhibit the body's ability to absorb iron by as much as 85%; drinking more than two cups of coffee a day has been implicated in calcium imbalance as well. A mild diuretic, caffeine can also cause you to lose potassium, magnesium and other minerals through your urine. Smoking or inhaling secondhand smoke interfers with your metabolism of B vitamins and more than doubles your vitamin C requirement.

References:

See Also:

Need more iron

Hormones

The ovaries serve the dual function of producing eggs and hormones. Progesterone is produced by the corpus luteum that develops from the follicle after the egg is shed. It prepares the uterus for successful implantation, growth of the embryo and maintenance of pregnancy. It is controlled in part by the central nervous system. Some environmental inputs can affect the secretions of gonadotropin hormones (estrogen, progesterone): rapid travel across time zones, stress, anxiety and other emotional changes. These inputs also influence the maturity of birth and may determine the occurence of premature birth. The pacemaker for rhythmic release of these hormones resides in the hypothalamus and the timekeeper for the slower monthly rhythm of the ovarian cycle resides in the ovary. Sources of food which balances female hormones contain omega fatty acids that can be found in fish products, flax seed, tofu and others. Birth pills can disrupt hormonal balance as well as other nutritional needs of the body such as magnesium, vitamin B6 and C and other nutrients.

The table below lists the effects of Estrogen and Progesterone on the reproductive tract.

Organ Estrogen Progesterone

Oviducts

lining muscular walls
increased cilia formation and activity increased contractility
increased secretion decreased contractility
increased secretion decreased contractility

Uterus
endometrium myometrium cervical glands
increased proliferation increased growth and contractility watery

secretions increased differentiation and secretion decreased contractility dense, viscous secretion (egg white consistency and stretchiness indicates ovulation coupled with increased body temp by as much as 1°F) increased differentiation and secretion decreased contractility dense, viscous secretion (egg white consistency and stretchiness indicates ovulation coupled with increased body temp by as much as 1°F) Breasts development of breasts stimulates stromal proliferation and fat deposition (some forms of breast cancer remain partially dependent on estrogen for growth)

Pelvis cause selective changes in bone structure such as widening of the pelvis w/c aids in the birth process

Vagina increased epithelial proliferation increased glycogen deposition increased differentiation decreased proliferation

Menstruation, the shedding of the endometrial lining is the result of the loss of estrogen and progesterone when the corpus luteum regresses. An ovarian cycle lasts about 28 days and consists of a follicular phase (~12- 14 days) in which the follicle grows to maturity, ovulation (~1 day), and a luteal phase (~12-14 days) in which the corpus luteum functions for its programmed lifespan. Herbs with Hormonal Effects

Chaste Tree/Vitex Active components are extracted from the dried, ripened fruits and the root bark of Vitex agnus-castus. The root bark has both free and conjugated forms of progesterone and hydroxyprogesterone which are also present in the leaves and flowers. Testosterone and epitestosterone were detected in the flower parts. The herb is claimed to have anti- inflammatory, antiandrogenic, progesterone-like, and antimicrobial effects. Recently isolated flavonoids exhibit antineoplastic activity and studies with rats have shown a hyperprolactinemia effect. It is also claimed to be useful for several endocrine and female reproductive tract disorders, including menstrual cycle regulation, uterine bleeding, ovarian insufficiency, aiding lactation, and combating acne.

Wild Yam Wild yam contains steroidal saponins, diosgenin, diosgenin, DHEA, phytosterols, alkaloids and tannins. DHEA, a constituent of wild yam, is a steroid hormone produced in the adrenal gland in humans; it is the most abundant adrenocorticoid hormone in the body. DHEA is believed to be useful in several conditions, including AIDS, Alzheimer's disease, CV disease, cancer, hypercholesterolemia, multiple sclerosis, obesity, psychological disorders and systemic lupus erythematosus. Wild yam is claimed to be useful in stomach and muscle cramps, menopausal symptoms, pain in the womb and ovaries and as an antispasmodic or diaphoretic.

See also: Postpartum Healing Ways

References: Johnson L. Essential Medical Physiology. Lippincott Raven Publisher, 1998 Northrup C. Women's Bodies, Women's Wisdom. Bantam Books, 1995

Breastfeeding Problems

Sore Nipples When my baby was about four weeks old, I saw a black spot on my nipple which seems to me dried blood. I felt pain every time the baby sucks my breast. I feel relieved after my midwife had shown me the right way the baby should suck on my breast and not on my nipple. I also applied breast milk itself and some Vitamin E. After a few days the soreness was gone. Constancia During the early weeks of breastfeeding, some mothers feel soreness in their nipples that may have blisters, crack or bleed. Be calm for nipple soreness will heal after a few weeks. The following should be noted:

Breast suck not nipple suck. The nipple and about one half of the areola should be well back in the baby's mouth. Bring the baby swiftly to the breast when the mouth is open wide enough. Press the baby's lower jaw to allow the baby's mouth to suck most of the areola.

Apply nipple care such as do not use soap or creams. Do not wash your nipples before the next feeding; nipple should be blotted dry and aired after feeding; apply scant amount of lanolin; do not wear any tight bra or wearing no bra at all; do not pull the baby's mouth when breaking the suction but place your little finger in the corner of the baby's mouth between the baby's gums.

Allow the Milk Ejection Reflex (MER) to occur by: relaxing; baby sucking the less sore breast first; hand expressing until the MER occurs; use varied breastfeeding positions to exert pressure on the less tender spot. Mastitis Stories

My CNM prescribed an antibiotic and echinacea, Vitamin E, chelated iron tabs, warm soaks for breasts, vitamin C, rests, proper positioning and Tylenol for fever. I wrap a cloth around my chest on the upper part of my breast which enables the breastmilk to slowly drip. She took a hot bath, massaged, used combing motion, took echinacea and ibuprofen, nursed the baby and it was still there, hard as can be. She thought it wasn't going to work, but she woke up in the morning and it was GONE! Nursing Herbs

To increase flow and supply: fennel, chamomile, bedstraw, hops, lavender, milkwort, blessed thistle, alfalfa, anise seed, fenugreek, sassafras, squaw vine To decrease flow: sage, parsley

Engorgement: marshmallow, comfrey Sore nipples: squaw vine poultice containing crushed squaw vine berries mixed with myrrh, almond oil, wheat germ oil, St. John's wort Breast infections: mulline, comfrey, lobelia, elder blossoms, apple cider vinegar, comfrey, echinacea Notes: Rice is used for weaning in the Philippines. Any solid foods are capable of decreasing the need for a baby to nurse. See also:

The Newborn after the Baby's Birth

Conscious Mothering/Parenting

If only mothers could see their babies through the babies' little eyes and feel their bodies every moment. Real attachment grows and unconditional love evolves. Every time we massage our babies and talk to them, we are helping them build trust and confidence in us. Having a good start in our pregnancies by talking to our baby inside our womb, gives us the right connection.

We might not know it, but we are actually passing positive energy or some spiritual touch to our unborn babies. My own experience with midwifery care strengthened my conscious mothering role. Midwifery standards of care includes proper nutrition, mother and infant massage, use of herbs and other natural remedies, partner's conscious participation from pregnancy and beyond, enlisting other support groups, care of women's bodies, empowering women and many more coping skills. As a new mother, we will be practicing conscious mothering using our own style and personality. Some of us have enough courage to birth at home, are more resourceful to find alternative ways and more determined to breastfeed even while working. I admit that my upbringing has shaped my mothering skills. There are many ways that we can allow human nature to work successfully. My mother is my role model in areas of childbirth for she birthed at home. Though I would not circumcise my child as she did as dictated by her society where circumcision was considered the male rite of passage into adulthood. We all try to find many ways to give the best to our babies. We can start by knowing the many alternative choices of caring for our babies and our bodies. When we are miles away from our mothers, we use other resources such as books, support groups, and classes. Communicate and connect with others for it can:

ease your pregnancy, labor, birthing and your entire mothering period. provide a sense of responsibility and belonging to other members of the family or groups of friends directly influence the child in the mother's womb

create a wholesome feeling about your body, your sexual desires, your capacity to birth and breastfeed your baby

heighten the relationship between partners and other members of the family during and after pregnancy

See also: Childbirth Education

Cultural Practices

One way of sharing the nurturing practices that we give to mothers and babies is through our cultural lifestyles and practices. Please email me at connie@motherhealth.com for other cultural practices that you know about concerning caring for women during their childbearing years.

In some rural places in the Philippines, a pregnant woman is a sign of blessings. She beings in good fortune. Children are considered as wealth. Families filled their homes with display of certificates or diplomas of their educated children. For poor families, children are viewed as source of income later on when they can earn for a living. The mother of a pregnant mother is the doula or the care giver after the baby is born. The father is viewed as always the provider. A midwife called "Komadrona" who attends to the birth. She or another person massage the mother during pregnancy, labor, and after delivering the baby. The midwife only needs boiled water to attend to the laboring mother.

After delivering the baby, the mother's stomach is wrapped by a piece of cloth and massaged every three days for two months to ensure that the uterus goes back to its proper place. Rice when served to the baby or red pepper applied to the nipples is used to wean the baby after a few years of nursing. The average year of nursing length is four years. The juice from a freshly cut young coconut is used as a supplemental food for the baby. It is also used during the last trimester of pregnancy to ease labor. The wish of a pregnant woman is always respected. She is not provoked or argued with since her emotions affect the unborn child. Herbs are used during pregnancy, labor, and postpartum.

The liquid from boiled guava leaves is used for cleansing the mother during postpartum. It serves as an antiseptic medication. Coconut oil is the most popularly used massage oil. Clams or any shell fish are served as soup to the mother during the last trimester of pregnancy and during nursing to increase the milk supply. The breast is also massaged during pregnancy to prepare the breast for nursing.

When in labor and the baby is breach (baby's head close to mom's heart), a massage therapist can bring the baby to its desired position, head first. Incense is used with the sitz bath remedy while the mother is wrapped in a hot towel during postpartum. A preparation with charcoal and herbs (indirectly applied to the mother's bottom) is used as the sitz bath itself. Boiled rain water is also used. Sex is resumed only after three months. In the cities of the Philippines, the same practice applies depending upon the availability of the lay midwife, massage therapist, and the environment.

In Taiwan, a postpartum mother is placed in a communal place with the care of doulas together with other postpartum mothers. For about two months, they are cared for. This kind of service exist solely for mothering the mother. In Ethiopia, the mother is also cared for the first three months during postpartum by relatives or helpers. Though circumcision for girls is still prevalent in some areas, educated women tend to do away with it.

In Russia, it is common to nurse more than one baby when supply is great. A mother who is in the same hospital room with other new mothers who also just delivered babies recalled how one mother volunteered to nurse her baby while her breast is still coping up with its supply of milk.

Advice from folks in the Philippines: You should not nap in the afternoon that long since you might have difficulty in delivering a bigger baby. Drink the juice of a young coconut for easy labor.

See Also: Emergency Childbirth

Discomfort during Pregnancy

Discomforts in your body tells you that your body is adjusting to the growing needs of the baby. Most of the common discomforts during pregnancy are caused by hormonal changes and/or anatomical changes such as enlarged uterus or engorged breasts. Listen to your body, slow down your hectic schedule, seek advice from midwives, mothers and other childbirth professionals.

Talk to your health care provider (doctor or midwife) often especially during your regular prenatal appointments so that you can learn the preventive measures. Examples of things that help prevent problems for you and your baby are: taking dietary supplements or herbs, changing in lifestyles or activities and learning about your body and the growing baby. Red raspberry leaf when taken as a tea is excellent in preparing the uterus for pregnancy, labor and birth. The following discomforts which may or may not be experienced by some women are arranged according to their major occurrence during pregnancy.

Back Pain To avoid or decrease back pain during your pregnancy, maintain a correct posture with the abdomen drawn in and the back and knees straight. Lifting heavy or awkward objects should be avoided during pregnancy if at all possible. When lifting, the objects must be held close to the body with the knees bent and the back kept straight to put the strain on the thigh

muscles and not those of the back. Pelvic rocks which combines hip movement and rocking the pelvis in back and forward motion helps tone the muscles and improve circulation. Pelvic tilts are also good for toning the muscles and ligaments that support the internal organs and easing tensions. Pelvic tilts are done by lying on your back with knees bent and feet flat. Tighten the abdominals and buttocks and press the small of the back down or scoop the sacrum into the floor repeatedly at least for 6 times or more and breathe. It can be done by either sitting, standing or lying. Massaging the lumbar region of the spine using long, deep and downward strokes eases low back pain. Most back tension releases really well by working the thumbs slowly and deeply along the long muscles of the spine, over the sacrum and through the buttocks. Sleeping on your sides provides relief for your back. Swimming during the last trimester especially offloads your body with the growing weight of the baby. In most countries in the Far East, women tend to spend more time squatting as they do their daily chores. Squatting, swimming and walking are good exercises. Massage is as common as bathing. A stroke or massage in the lower back with massage oil such as olive, calendula, almond or coconut oil helps backache problems. Check your doctor or care giver for kidney problems. "If back pains increase or get worse, or you are experiencing kidney pain, check with your health care providers. Sometimes women have kidney stones or muscle spasms during pregnancy. And of course, any sort of persistent or intermittent low back pain could indicate preterm labor, or possibly an infection." Pat Sonnenstuhl, CNM

Universal Herbs for Back Pain: Minerals such as Calcium (Chamomile, Fennel), Cobalt (Dandelion, Red Clover), Iron (Yellow Dock, Rosemary, Ginseng, Burdock), Magnesium (Alfalfa, Catnip, Red Clover, Valerian), Vitamin K (Rose hips, Cayenne), Zinc (Licorice, Sarsaparilla) and Vitamin C (Bee pollen, chickweed, comfrey, Echinacea, garlic, juniper berries, peppermint, Saluyot in the Philippines and rose hips).

Nausea and Vomiting

Extreme nausea of pregnancy seems to be related to the very high levels of the pregnancy hormones some women experience during the first few months of pregnancy. And these hormones maintain their proper balance by about the fourth month of pregnancy.

A light full body massage oxygenates the body. I experienced nausea and vomiting during my second pregnancy with my daughter. Taking ginger capsule and eating crackers early in the morning before getting up from my bed helped me. The combination of walking, fresh air, avoiding greasy or highly seasoned foods, using the power of the mind, and relaxing also helped in controlling nausea and vomiting. Eat small, frequent meals and dry foods with fluids between meals.

I know of a friend who took birth control pills for a long time and then experienced extreme nausea and vomiting during her pregnancy. Sometimes taking birth control pills before pregnancy can deplete a woman of the B vitamins, so these need to be added to the diet .Vitamin B6 100 mg can be very helpful taken two or three times a day. My midwife's advice is to eat nuts since they stay longer in the stomach because of their high protein content. In Europe, mothers apply ice cold washcloth to their eyes when nauseous. Drinking lots of water and eating something (in small amounts) every two hours also prevents nausea and vomiting. In China, acupuncture points on the wrists (or sea bands) can help in nausea. If vomiting persists longer than 24 hours be sure you discuss this with your health care provider. They might have other suggestions, or might want to do some specific tests to rule out more serious conditions.

Universal Herbs for Nausea: Ginger and Vitamin B6 (Hawthorne, Licorice, Papaya), peach leaf, blackberries, red raspberry, peppermint, wild yam, anise, cinnamon, cloves, oregano. The lemon scent sometimes helps women get through this difficult time.

Heartburn and Gas Eat small, more frequent meals. Lie down and do abdominal breathing. Try some pelvic rocks. Pay attention to which foods and spices bring on heartburn and gas. Check your food combination (fruit with heavy protein is not good) and avoid overeating. Avoid offending foods such as fatty and friend foods, beans, tofu, carbonation, etc. Eat papaya. If you get pain after eating spicy foods, perhaps your gallbladder is acting up. Again, persistent pain of any type needs to be reported to your health care provider. Universal Herbs: Angelica, borage, cayenne, peppermint, valerian, wintergreen, holy thistle, papaya Constipation

Caused by decreased motility of the digestive system, drinking lots of fluids and eating lots of fiber can help prevent constipation. Avoid laxatives. Try prunes, prune juice or carrot juice. Eat plenty of raw greens and bran which are high fiber foods and any fresh and dried fruits. Eat banana in moderation. Drink a lot of fluids especially water. Exercise daily. Squat on the toilet or use a box or stool for elevating feet to facilitate bowel movements. Develop regular bowel habits.

Hemorrhoids Closely related to constipation is hemorrhoids. Some of the same

suggestions apply: Rub Vitamin E oil directly on the anus. Eat lots of fruits. A mother in the Far East cautions from over eating spicy foods, intoxicating liquors, white bread, sugar, fried foods and all acid-forming foods which cause fermentation. Drink at least a pint of fresh fruit or vegetable juice each day. Avoid taking ordinary purgatives that are on the market as they irritate the membranous lining of the bowels and intestines.

Drink more fluids. Put feet on a small stool while sitting on the toilet for bowel movement. Do pelvic rocks and lots of pelvic floor exercises. Take sitz baths (shallow and hot for the parts of you where you sits). Apply witch hazel or a commercial preparation and rectal poultice of chamomile leaves and white oak bark powder. Try to lie down or at least get off your feet part of the day. Gently tuck the hemorrhoid back up into the rectum with a lubricated finger for instant relief.

Herbs: ginger, witch hazel (external), burdock, plaintain, yarrow For external suppository, mix the following with glycerine, stiff enough to form suppository and insert it into the rectum at night and leaving it: 2 oz of powdered Hemlock Bark, 1 oz of Golden Seal, 1 oz of powdered wheat flour of almond, rice, or corn of almond, rice, or corn, 1 oz of Boric acid, 1 oz of Bayberry bark Bleeding Gums

Be certain you are not anemic, and be very gentle on your gums during pregnancy. Use a soft toothbrush. Increase your intake of Vitamin C and calcium. Floss regularly and see your dentist. Try applying white oak bark powder to your gums or use white oak bark tea for swishing around on the inside of the mouth. Brush with equal parts of golden seal and myrrh three times a day.

Herbs: Shepherd's purse and wild alum root Mild Blood Pressure

Lie on your left side and have someone massage you with slow, firm hand. Relaxation can help lower an elevated blood pressure. Eat foods containing garlic, ginger and onions. Swelling/Ankle Edema

Lying on your side or elevating your feet can help relieve swelling and edema. Sitting or standing for long periods of time can promote edema. Dring lots of fluids to promote good tissue balance. Soaking in the bathtub can help relive the edema too. Putting your feet up, high fluid intake. Eating plenty of protein rich food. are important. Consult your health care provider if you have sudden edema, blinding headaches or there is protein in the urine coupled with a high blood pressure and swelling. Insomia

Do a facial (around the eyes, the jaw and the top of the neck beneath the occiput), head and neck massage before going to bed. Drink chamomile tea and use lots of pillows. Eat some protein and avioid sugary foods at bedtime. Some women find a cup of hot chocolate milk helps them sleep. Keep food at the side of your bed should you be hungry in the middle of the night. Leg Cramps

Press the point in the center of the calf for relief. Also, flex the foot towards you with hard pressure or dorsiflex foot to stretch affected muscle. Eat calcium rich foods and take a calcium/magnesium supplement before going to bed. Sleeping on the right or left side helps (with lots of pillows for support) prevent leg cramps and doesn't impede the blood vessels responsible for baby's oxygenation.

Varicose Veins Do not massage directly and deeply on a swollen vein. Superficial, general massage toward the heart is helpful and preventative. Red spiderlike veins are broken blood vessels not varicose veins and can be massaged. If the area becomes painful, tender or swoolen, notify your health care provider. Some women with varicose veins in the vaginal area are helped by wearing knit bicycle pants which provide good support for the vaginal area. Arrange frequent opportunities to put your legs up to promote improved blood flow. Urinary Frequency

Continue to drink at least 8 glasses of water, and go to the bathroom frquently. Frequency is caused in early pregnancy by the uterus pressing on the bladder with a growing fetus. Towards the end of pregnancy, it's usually the baby's head

Dyspnea/Shortness of breath This is usually related to the increased levels of fluids your body is producing. At mid pregnancy you are carrying about 50% more fluids than when you are not pregnant. Some of this is within your body tissues, and some are contributed by your amniotic fluid. Maintain proper posture when sitting and standing. When sleeping on either sides, prop up on pillows on both sides. If you smoke, decrease or stop smoking, as this decreases good oxygenation to you and your baby.

Increased Vaginal Discharge Bath daily and avoid douching, nylon panty hose/underpants. Wear cotton underwear. If you have a cheesy discharge or yeast infection, cut on your sugar intake and wash with diluted vinegar or tea tree oil (Tea tree oil has antibacterial and antifungal activity in vitro). After urinating, always clean from your vagina back towards your rectum.

See Also:

Doula

If you happen to find out about any doula (lay labor support) services in your area, please email me (connie@motherhealth.com) so that we can compile a list of names for other moms. Doulas support the laboring mother and provide varied services from childbirth education to postpartum support. They support the mother in all aspects of her pregnancy. Studies have shown reduced cesaerean operations among mothers who have doulas with them before and during birth. In the absence of a midwife or nurse midwife in the hospital, Doulas are there to be mom's advocate in the birthing experience she so desires. I provide doula services in the Silicon Valley area and you may email me if you are personally interested. Doulas can help shorten labor and be your ally in the hospital. They can help create miracles for birthing families.

See also: A poem for mothers

Emergency Childbirth

Emergency Childbirth: When Baby Arrives Before the Midwife or Doctor Most births are spontaneous and normal. The baby is crafted for survival. Relax and do the following after contacting the midwife or doctor who is on her way:

1. Move her to a comfortable place away from the toilet. Call for help.
2. Make sure the room is warm and draft free. Remember that baby needs a warm environment. A clean, dry towel and a hat should be ready for the baby.
3. Prepare a bowl of warm water with provolone iodine solution and a clean cloth in it. Place a clean under pad under the mother with the paper side next to her skin. Place another empty bowl (to catch the placenta later on) in close proximity together with scissors, gauze, bulb syringe and cord clamp. Put all items gathered on a clean towel.
4. Wash your hands thoroughly. Tear open several packs of 4 x 4's sterile gauze. Put gloves on if available.
5. As the head starts emerging, put gentle counter pressure against the bulging perineum. Don't touch anything except the mother and baby so as not to contaminate. As the baby's head starts emerging, remind the mother that she will feel the "ring of fire" which is normal.

6. Place a gauze 4 x 4 over the mother's anus, to prevent contamination. wipe the feces away, if necessary, and place a clean 4 x 4 over the anus. Make sure you don't contaminate the gloves or your hands.

7. Ask the mother to pant as the head crowns and is born. Support the mother's perineum with both hands.

8. When head is out, slide your fingers in along the baby's neck to feel for the umbilical cord. If you feel the cord, try slipping it over the baby's head. If you can't, it's usually not a problem to leave it, unless it is too tight and keeps the baby from coming out.

9. If the cord is very tight: with your fingers placed between the baby's neck and cord, clamp with two hemostats or two cord clamps in two spots an inch apart.

10. Make sure you put both clamps on next to each other on the same piece of cord. Carefully cut between the two clamps and unwind the cord from baby's neck. Keep both clamps on and be sure they are clamped tightly.

11. If the bag of waters is still around the baby's face, as it is born, tear the bag by pinching it apart with your fingers.

12. Wipe the baby's face with a gauze 4 x 4. Use the syringe to suction the baby, if needed. While keeping the bulb syringe squeezed, gently place the tip (sweeping from the side) in baby's mouth and release the bulb syringe. Spray contents onto a gauze 4 x 4. Do the same for both nostrils.

13. Ask the mother to push as the baby rotates to face one of the mother's leg. With one hand under baby's head and the other on top of it, exert gentle pressure downward pressure on the baby's head to facilitate the delivery of the top shoulder.

14. When the top shoulder is out about two or three inches, lift upward on the baby's head to help the bottom shoulder come out. The baby's body will follow. Hold the baby (with her/his face down) with your two hands since the baby is slippery.

15. Place the baby on mother's belly with mom lying on her back and both in tummy to tummy position. Cover the baby and put her/his hat on. Make sure you don't pull the umbilical cord.

16. As soon as the cord stops pulsating, you can cut the cord. Attach cord clamp securely 1/2 inch from baby's belly button. Place gauze

under the cord. Cut cord 1/2 inch away from the clamp on the other side (away from the baby).

17. Baby should be pink. If baby is bluish, white or limp and not crying, do the following: Run your fingers up the baby's spine, massaging vigorously. Flick baby's feet with your fingers. Having mother talk to baby, continue the above. Keep baby warm and dry.

18. If baby is still not responding and it has been one minute since birth, begin mouth to mouth resuscitation with gentle puffs from your cheeks. Keep baby warm and dry and have someone call the emergency personnel.

19. Watch for signs that the placenta is detaching such as a gush of blood, the cord gets longer and mother feels more contractions.

20. When the above happens: wrap gauze around section of the cord, so it's not so slick. Place opposite hand against mother's pubic bone and press gently inward and upward. Ask mother to give little push with the next contraction. using gentle cord traction, guide the cord downward as you see the placenta start to emerge, lift upward with the cord to help placenta out.

21. Wipe and warm the baby by wrapping the baby well and putting the baby on mother's breast, apply CPR if necessary, wait for the midwife or doctor to cut the cord, let the mother massage her uterus and stay with the mother.

See Also: Fathers

Fathers

The art of fathering comes from experience and through modeling from the nurturing skills of mothers before us. When you and your partner work together from the moment of conception (i.e., attending childbirth classes together, interviewing care givers like doctors/midwives) till the baby is growing and needing both of your time, your mothering is easy and your marriage grows stronger. The father will also feel that joyful sacrifice that you feel. He will then understand why you behave in such way and how to be there at the right time for you and your baby. Fathers are also like expectant mothers, anxious of their new role as fathers. They are now serious in making more money for the new addition to the family. They view themselves as provider and giver of financial stability. Frequently, because everyone is thinking As everyone thinks of the mother's needs, the father is left on his own to fulfill his own emotional needs. He usually senses the need to be involved with own the birth of the baby and take part in the unfolding of this new life, but sometimes isn't just what he can and should do. He needs affirmation and praise for the work he does and the involvement he has. Knows that he should also be patted on his back for he needs the reassurance that everything will work well. We should accept the many roies of our partner, the father of our babies, and learn to accept them where they are in their own parenting and fathering roles. "I remember one father telling me how left out he felt of the breastfeeding experience, especially in the baby's first few months of life. As his child grew, he saw things he could do, and was a wonderful, nurturing father. It is a wonderful, joyous and challenging learning experience for all." Pat Sonnenstuhl, CNM

The various roles a father takes in pregnancy, labor, birth and afterwards are: provider, birth assistant, massage therapist, health care giver at home, lover, nurturer, companion, friend and the list goes on and on. Today's fathers are more involved than ever in caring for their families and that the positive effect of their involvement touched all aspects of their lives. They were more likely to have successful careers, happy marriages, and to be leaders in the community. And their kids shared the success - sons and daughters of supportive fathers enjoyed more success in school and work. An expectant father's feelings should be validated in the same way we validate a mother's feelings. After all, family-centered birth will drive the trend towards a more humane way of birthing, the real American way of birth. To My Postpartum Wife

I am your partner, the father of our baby

I would like to care for our baby if not as much as you do I wouldn't like to see our baby given up to strange baby sitters I wouldn't like to see you cook, clean house, do the laundry or entertain You will be given a helper, a doula, or an assistant If not on our bed, you will be sitting on your rocking chair, wearing your nursing gown when resting You shall honor me with my share of household chores Take long walks in places with clean air, eat healthy food and drink much water and juice Welcome with you friendly and helpful visitors with good baby advice. Sleep when baby sleeps so that your nursing will go unimpeded. I am your husband and I will give you the energy and environment conducive for both you and our baby. Your partner in love, at your service

See also: Having sex before and after the baby is born

Letter from a Midwife

Dear Connie, I often wonder just where to begin the discussion of homebirth, natural birth and the powers of women's bodies. Sometimes the goal is only to get people to agree that homebirth is a safe choice for those who choose it period. There is no use trying to get a Republican to become part of the Green party. We can only take baby steps to educate and spread the truth. Let us remember three out of four babies are born at home in the world. The U.S.A. mortality rate is astonishingly high for a "1st world" country. Labeling childbirth as painful and frightening is buying into the medical model. Pregnancy is not an illness and birth needs no management. Our bodies may be corporeal but they are not savage and feeling their sensations is a pleasure and quite empowering. Keep spreading the word Connie. Birth is as safe as life gets.

Erin Ryan, Certified Nurse Midwife

Having Sex before and after the baby is born

The sexual hormones during pregnancy is high. The woman's body is warmer during pregnancy because of the growing fetus inside her and her tissues are very sensitive. Having sex before the baby is chemically beneficial especially during the last trimester since the semen is rich in prostaglandin, an essential hormone which stimulates labor. Eating fish which is rich in omega fatty acids also stimulates the production of prostaglandin. In a hospital birth a prostaglandin gel is sometimes applied to the cervix to ripen it and initiate labor. Sex after the baby's birth should not happen until the sixth week after the baby was born or until the mother's tissues are healed and she is comfortable to make love again. It is interesting to note the different feelings of pregnant women about their interest in sex. "During the last trimester of pregnancy, I feel uncomfortable because of the size of my belly. I still feel the same interest in sex the whole length of my pregnancy. I just have to communicate a lot with my partner regarding my feelings when making love. Overall, my interest in sex increased throughout pregnancy maybe because I don't have to worry about unwanted pregnancy and plus my partner finds me more warm." Veronica, Russia

"I think giving birth and making love both require intimacy. This is one reason why I wanted a woman to assist me in birthing my baby. I became so focused when I delivered my baby in my house with my husband. I have the same calming attitude in birthing the baby as in making love." Divina, Philippines "My sexuality and interest in making love disappeared during the last trimester for fear that it may affect the baby." Rose, California "My size in the last trimester made intercourse difficult. Thanks to one article about ways of making love when pregnant, it made it easier for me and my husband." Cristy, Bulgaria

"Wives' bodies should always serve their husbands. That is our culture." Hana, Ethiopia

See also: Midwives

Women's Bodies

Healing Ways for a Cut and an Episiotomy

Care for episiotomies and tears cold sanitary pads or sitz bath with equal amount of (three tablespoons) witch hazel astringent and herbs solution containing comfrey leaf/root, uva ursi, golden seal, sage, myrrh, salt.

drinking liquid every hour or 30 minutes after birth; eating foods that will not constipate; drink prune juice.

stand for a while hours after birth; exposing to air and sun few minutes 15-20 minutes in the morning and afternoon.

See Also: Postpartum Healing Ways

Herbs and Nutrition

Homebirth

Why Homebirth with Midwives? The desire for the strongest possible bonding between newborn and family. Family-centered care during and after pregnancy. The desire to be in control of the birth without unnecessary medical intervention. The personal satisfaction derived from the care of midwives and chosen attendants. The continuity of care and personal touch they afford. The comforting and familiar setting of home.

The related benefits derived from homebirth such as ease of getting started in breastfeeding, the use of herbal remedies, safer procedures that respects a woman's body, the use of massage/acupressure and many more holistic healing ways.

Homebirth reduces stress and anxiety by: providing a relaxed, safe, and comfortable place for the patient to undergo labor in encouraging the patient to be in control of her labor allowing the patient to have supportive, loving people around her allowing the patient to walk around, to eat, and drink and to choose the most comfortable position during labor practicing relaxation techniques to reduce stress ensuring constant attendance by the midwife or physician and attendants assisting in the labor and delivery.

Statistics The rate of Caesarean (major abdominal surgeries) operations is very low for midwives and homebirths, compared to hospital births. Part of the reason for this low rate is the fact that most homebirths are not high risk. But more importantly, midwives aren't in a hurry. They do not have the institutional time pressures that come along with hospital births. And, it has never been shown that shorter labors are safer than longer ones. For midwives, labor and childbirth are a natural process and, unless distress to the mother or baby is indicated, this process is not interfered with through drugs, medical equipment or Caesarean operation. Homebirth allows for the full participation of family members. Under the guidance and assistance of a midwife, the opportunity is available for husbands or partners to "catch" their child as it is born. These moments can be very powerful and transformational in the lives of new parents.

Babies

At homebirths, babies are immediately placed on the mom's stomach or breast, providing security, warmth and immediate bonding between mom and baby. This contact provides an additional measure of security for both mom and baby.

Family At homebirths, family and friends frequently join together in support of the birthing family. Husbands or partners may be very important to the birthing mom during this time. The midwife can help fill the primary support role if other support is not available to a single mom. Usually someone other than the mom or her partner assumes responsibility for any children who are present, freeing mom to focus on birthing. Another adult may be a designated photographer if desired.

Midwife The midwife helps to calm people who are present at the birth. Tension in a room can slow down or stop a labor. The midwife manages these situations so the mom and her partner can continue to focus on the birthing process. The personal touch and the continuity of care of a midwife is very valuable especially for the first time mother who needs to know how to start breastfeeding, care for her baby and her body. Because homebirth families are well prepared, the birthing process can feel quite natural. They can let go of any fear surrounding birth and trust the process instead. If difficulties occur along the way, they are calmly resolved. During labor the partner and family nurture the mom. The midwife is watchful for any complications or signs of distress in either the mom or the baby. Throughout labor, the midwife asks permission to perform various procedures and explains to the mom and family what she is doing and why.

Birthing Process The birthing process is allowed to take its own course and set its own pace. The general philosophy is that any interventions (administering drugs or trying to hurry things along) can create more harm than good. In the safety and security of her own home, the mom is likely to be less inhibited about trying different labor positions and locations.

She can sit on the toilet or go for a walk outside. She can eat or drink whatever she wants. She writes her own script. When it's time to deliver, she can often try whatever position she wants: on her side, squatting, sitting or kneeling.

Complications Occasionally, there will be complications during labor. The midwife is trained to recognize early stages of complications and to take necessary action. Transport to the hospital during the course of the birthing process may be necessary for the health of either the mother or baby.

To promote a smooth transition in this situation, some midwives have their pregnant moms pre-register at a nearby hospital. Husbands or other designated individuals are advised on directions to the hospital, as well as to have fuel in the car, or other means of transport pre-arranged. An often overlooked point is for the car to be equipped with a proper infant seat to facilitate the return trip from the hospital.

In the rare case when the baby has difficulty breathing on its own, midwives are fully trained in infant CPR. Usually, putting the baby right to the breast and having mom talk to her baby will encourage it to take those first breaths.

Postpartum Putting the baby immediately to the breast helps reduce any bleeding the mom may have. The sucking action stimulates the uterus and causes it to contract. This closes off blood vessels and reduces bleeding.

The first moments of interactions between mother and baby are a sacred time, a time to be honored. This is baby's special bonding time with its parents and all the family and friends present. When a baby is born, all that baby wants is to be loved and taken care of. This early bonding allows them to relax and feel secure. The midwife makes sure that the needs of the mother and baby during postpartum (after birth) are met.

Breastmilk The mother's milk supply usually comes on the third or fourth day after birth. Prior to that, the baby is drinking a substance called colostrum, which has many antibodies to help fight bacteria and build up the baby's immune system. It is also rich in vitamins and protein. The midwife will offer encouragement and support in getting started to successfully breastfeed. Infections

Some members of the medical community have recently acknowledged that having a homebirth decreases the mother's and baby's chances of contracting an infection. The mother is used to the bacteria in her own environment and has built up immunities to it. This is passed on to the baby through the colostrum. Even when women are segregated in maternity wards, infections are much more commonplace after hospital births than homebirths. A mother who is tired after a Caesarian operation could not attend to her baby during the first hour of the baby's life and during her own healing process.

One of the benefits of homebirth is that after the birth and special bonding time, mom and baby can be tucked into their own bed in the comfort of their home to rest and sleep. The husband or partner can join them for rest and deeper bonding.

Commitment and Responsible Parenthood The most successful homebirthers are those who have a strong commitment to it and who trust in their body's natural ability to birth. They are often willing to devote time and energy to finding the right birth practitioner, to doing their own research, attend childbirth classes, and to take better care of themselves through proper nutrition, conscious living and making the choices that are good for the baby and mom. Family-centered Care

Homebirths with midwives have the following in common: no electronic fetal monitors no IVs to keep mom hydrated no artificial rupture of membranes

no forceps or vacuum extractors, even with long pushing phases no inductions for "failure to progress", even with long pushing phases no drugs of any kind before the baby's birth no episiotomies no one hollered at the mom to PUSH as pushing is self-directed, according to the mom's urge to bear down.

no separation in the new family after birth no routine suctioning of babies; only if needed no cord cutting until well after delivery of the placenta no limit on food, drinks, numbers of people present, positions, and other holistic birthing ways And best of all, mothers get to birth in their own way, in their own time, in the place they feel most comfortable. This is how we should welcome our babies.

See also: Doula

Studies: RECENT BRITISH MEDICAL JOURNAL THAT FEATURED
HOMEBIRTH

REFERENCES

British Medical Journal editorial 1996 "Home birth, Safe in selected women, and with adequate infrastructure and support" British Medical Journal vol 313, No 7068, pp 1276-7.

Davies J, et al 1996

"Prospective regional study of planned home birth" British Medical Journal vol 313, No 7068, pp 1302 - 6

Northern Region Perinatal Mortality Survey Group 1996

"Collaborative survey of perinatal loss in planned and unplanned home births"

British Medical Journal vol 313, No 7068, pp 1306 - 9

Wiegers T et al 1996 "Outcome of planned home and planned hospital births in low risk

pregnancies: prospective study in midwifery practices in the Netherlands"

British Medical Journal vol 313, No 7068, pp 1309 - 1313

AcKermann-Liebrich U. et al 1996 "Home versus Hospital deliveries: follow up study of matched pairs for

procedures and outcome" British Medical Journal Vol 313, No 7068, pp 1313 - 1318

MORE REFERENCES

Abel S. Kearns RA. Department of Anthropology, University of Auckland, New Zealand

"Birth places: a geographical perspective on planned home birth in New Zealand"

Social Science & Medicine. 33(7):825-34, 1991.

Ackermann-Liebrich U et al 1994 "Comparing home to hospital deliveries: Recruitment, referrals and neonatal outcome"

Soz Praventivmed Vol 39, No 1, pp 28

Albers LL. Katz VL. University of Medicine and Dentistry of New Jersey

"Birth setting for low-risk pregnancies. An analysis of the current literature"

Journal of Nurse-Midwifery. 36(4):215-20, 1991 Jul-Aug.

van Alten R et al 1989 "Midwifery in the Netherlands; The Wormerveer Study"

British Journal of Obstetrics & Gynaecology, Vol 96, No 6, pp 656 - 662

Anderson R. Greener D A descriptive analysis of home births attended by CNMs in two

nurse-midwifery services Journal of Nurse-Midwifery. 36(2):95-103, 1991 Mar-Apr.

Bortin S. Alzugaray M. Dowd J. Kalman J.

Santa Cruz Women's Health Center, California "A feminist perspective on the study of home birth. Application of a

midwifery care framework" Journal of Nurse-Midwifery. 39(3):142-9, 1994 May-Jun.

Buitendijk, S 1994

"How safe are Dutch home births?" In: Abrahams E (ED) Successful Home Birth and Midwifery - the

Dutch Model Bergen, Garvey and Greenwood, Westport CT, USA

Burnett C, Jones J, Rooks J, et al.

Home delivery and neonatal mortality in North Carolina. JAMA Vol 244, No 24 2741-45 1980

Campbell R & McFarlane A 1987 "Where to be born, the debate and the evidence"

National Perinatal Epidemiology Unit, Oxford, UK

Campbell R et al 1984 "Home birth in England and Wales, perinatal mortality according to intended place of birth" British Medical Journal, vol 289, pp 721-24

Chamberlain M. Soderstrom B. Kaitell C. Stewart P

"Consumer interest in alternatives to physician-centred hospital birth in Ottawa"

Midwifery. 7(2):74-81, 1991 Jun.

Damstra-Wijmenga S 1984 "Home confinement: the positive results in Holland"

Journal Royal College of General Practitioners, vol 34, pp 425-30

Davis-Floyd RE Birth as an American Right of Passage

Davis-Floyd RE.

Department of Anthropology, University of Texas at Austin 78712 "The technocratic body: American childbirth as cultural expression."

[Review] Social Science & Medicine. 38(8): 1125-40, 1994 Apr.

Declercq E

Merrimack College, North Andover, Massachusetts "Where babies are born and who attends their births: findings from the

revised 1989 United States Standard Certificate of Live Birth" Obstetrics & Gynecology. 81(6):997-1004, 1993 Jun.

Durand A The safety of home birth: the Farm study

American Journal of Public Health Vol 82 No 3 450-53 1992

Ford C. Iliffe S. Franklin O. Department of Primary Health Care, Whittington Hospital, London

"Outcome of planned home births in an inner city practice" British Medical Journal vol 303(6816):1517-9, 1991 Dec 14.

Hafner-Eaton C. Pearce LK., Oregon State University

"Birth choices, the law, and medicine: balancing individual freedoms and protection of the public's health."

Journal of Health Politics, Policy & Law. 19(4):813-35, 1994 Winter.

Hinds M et al 1985 "Neonatal outcome in planned versus unplanned out-of-hospital births in

Kentucky" JAMA Vol 253 pp 1578 - 82

Janssen PA. Holt VL. Myers SJ

"Licensed midwife-attended, out-of-hospital births in Washington state: are they safe?"

Birth. 21(3):141-8, 1994 Sep. Kenny P. King MT. Cameron S. Shiell A

"Satisfaction with postnatal care--the choice of home or hospital" Midwifery. 9(3):146-53, 1993 Sep.

MacVicar J. Dobbie G. Owen-Johnstone L. Jagger C. Hopkins M. Kennedy J. Department of Obstetrics & Gynaecology, Leicester Royal Infirmary, UK

"Simulated home delivery in hospital: a randomised controlled trial" British Journal of Obstetrics & Gynaecology. 100(4):316-23, 1993 Apr.

Mathews JJ. Zadak K. Loyola University Medical Center, Maywood, IL 60163

"The alternative birth movement in the United States: history and current status"

Women & Health. 17(1):39-56, 1991.

Mehl L et al 1977 "Outcomes of elective home births, a series of 1,146 case"

Journal Reprod. Medicine vol 19, pp 281-90

Olesen 0 1997 "A Meta-analysis of the safety of home birth"

Journal of Birth, March 1997

Olsen O. Afdeling for Social Medicin, Kobenhavns Universitet

[Home delivery and scientific reasoning]. [Norwegian] [Source] Tidsskrift for Den Norske Laegeforening. 114(30):3655-7,

1994 Dec 10.

Pearse W 1987 "Partuition, places and priorities"

American Journal of Public Health vol 77, pp 923 - 24

Sakala C. Health Policy Institute, Boston University, MA 02215

"Midwifery care and out-of-hospital birth settings: how do they reduce unnecessary cesarean section births?"

Social Science & Medicine. 37(10):1233-50, 1993 Nov.

Schramm W et al 1987 "Neonatal mortality in Missouri home births 1978-1984"

American Journal of Public Health vol 77,no 8 pp 930-35

Shearer JML 1985

"Five year prospective survey of risk of booking for a home birth in Essex"

British Medical Journal vol 291 pp 1478 - 80

van Steensel-Moll HA. van Duijn CM. Valkenburg HA. van Zanen GE. Department of Epidemiology and Biostatistics,

Erasmus University Medical School, Rotterdam, The Netherlands

Tyson H

Outcomes of 1001 midwife-attended home births in Toronto, 1983-1988 Birth. 18(1):14-9, 1991 Mar.

Wagner M.

Pursuing the Birth Machine: the Search for Appropriate Birth Technology. ACE Graphics, Sydney 1994

Wagner, Marsden

"A Global Witch-hunt" Lancet vol 346 pp.1020-1022; Oct. 14, 1995.

Woodcock HC. Read AW. Bower C. Stanley FJ. Moore DJ

"A matched cohort study of planned home and hospital births in Western Australia 1981-1987"

Midwifery. 10(3):125-35, 1994 Sep.

INFANT MASSAGE

Touch and massage are simple forms of communication. The baby's skin is more sensitive than that of an adult. Massage lightly with the surface of your fingers and palm. Start from the hands and feet. Use calendula oil or another natural, light oil such as Almond or Arnica oil. This oil can be used as postnatal care:

- loosen and relaxes the new baby
- gently removes the cradle cap on baby's head
- protects baby's delicate skin

Other aromatherapy oil for postnatal care can consist of St John's Wort, Arnica, Calendula oil, Betula, Vitamin E and pure essential oils of Chamomile, Lavender, Rosemary, sweet Almond and Olive oils. See also: Breastfeeding

Pregnancy Humor
Please email (connie@motherhealth.com) me if you have any humor related to pregnancy and baby care that you wish to share with others.

QUESTION ANSWER

Am I more likely to get pregnant if my husband wears boxers rather than briefs?

Yes, but you'll have an even better chance if he doesn't wear anything at all.

What do you call a pregnancy that begins while using birth control?

A misconception.

What is the difference between a Direct Entry Midwife (DEM) and a Certified Nurse Midwife (CNM)?

Seven years of education for CNM and at least seven years of apprenticeship for DEM.

Can a woman get pregnant from a toilet seat?

Yes, but the baby would be awfully funny looking.

What is the easiest way to figure out exactly when I got pregnant?

Have sex once a year.

What is a chastity belt? A labor-saving device.

What is the most common pregnancy craving?

For men to be the ones who get pregnant.

I normally wear a size 34-C bra. Now that I'm pregnant, should I continue to wear a bra?

Not if you don't mind switching in the future to a size 34-Long.

What is the most reliable method to determine a baby's sex?

Childbirth.

My blood type is type O-positive and my husband's is A-negative. What if my baby is born, say, type AB-positive?

Then the jig is up.

Should I have a baby after 35 (no need for unnecessary tests if you think you are healthy)?

No, 35 children is enough

My husband and I are very attractive. I'm sure our baby will be beautiful enough for commercials. Whom should I contact about this?

Your therapist.

I'm two months pregnant now. When will my baby move?

With any luck, right after he finishes college.

How would I know that my bag of waters When you taste it and it is not

broke? salty.

How will I know if my vomiting is morning sickness or the flu?

If it's the flu, you'll get better.

My brother tells me that since my husband has a big nose, and genes for big noses are dominant, my baby will have a big nose as well. Is this true?

The odds are greater that your brother will have a fat lip.

Does pregnancy affect a woman's memory?

I don't remember.

Since I became pregnant, my breasts, rear end, and even my feet have grown. Is there anything that gets smaller during pregnancy?

Yes, your bladder and your brain (latest research according to a CAT scan).

Ever since I've been pregnant, I haven't been able to go to bed at night without onion rings. Is this a normal craving?

Depends on what your doing with them.

The more pregnant I get, the more often strangers smile at me. Why?

A. Cause your fatter than they are.

My wife is five months pregnant and so moody that sometimes she's borderline irrational.

So what's your question?

Will I love my dog less when the baby is born?

No, but your husband might get on your nerves.

Under what circumstances can sex at the end of pregnancy (semen contains prostaglandin - hormone, which stimulate labor) bring on labor?

When the sex is between your husband and another woman.

What's the difference between a nine- months pregnant woman and a Playboy centerfold?

Nothing, if the pregnant woman's husband knows what's good for him.

What position should the baby be in during the ninth month of pregnancy?

Head down, pressing firmly on your bladder.

What's the best way to get a man to give up his seat to a pregnant woman?

Brute force.

When is the best time to get an epidural (drug injected to mom or added in the IV that depresses the baby and slows labor for some mothers)?

Right after you find out you are pregnant.

Is there any reason I have to be in the Not unless the word "alimony" delivery room while my wife is in labor? means anything to you.

How long is the average woman in labor (it takes 10-30 minutes for some second- time mothers)?

Whatever she says, divided by two.

I'm modest. Once I'm in the hospital to deliver, who will see me in that delicate position?

Authorized personnel only--- doctors, nurses, odorless, photographers, florists, cleaning crews, journalists, etc.

What does it mean when the baby's head is crowning (burning sensation in mom's puss signaling the baby's head is coming out)?

It means you feel as though not only a crown but the entire throne is trying to make it's way out of you.

What are forceps (metal that pulls baby out since mom can't push after she is given drugs for pain relief or other measures)?

Giant baby tweezers.

Does anyone in this country still give birth in the fields or in a van?

Not on purpose.

Is there anything I should avoid while recovering from childbirth?

Yes, pregnancy.

Does labor cause hemorrhoids? Labor causes anything you want to blame it for.

Under what circumstances should a baby not be circumcised (baby's foreskin has about six functional nerves)?

When it's a girl, for starters.

Is there a safe alternative to breast pumps?

Yes, baby lips.

Why is standing the best position when delivering a breech baby (feet first)?

Gravity.

Why does is take some time to deliver a baby boy than a baby girl even when in squatting position?

Wider chest circumference for boys.

When would I know the day that true labor comes?

When your weight is about half a pound less.

What does it mean when a baby is born with teeth?

It means that the baby's mother may want to rethink her plans to nurse.

Why is nipple stimulation used to induce labor?

It releases the sex hormones which initiate labor.

How does one sanitize nipples? Bathe daily and wear a clean bra.

It beats boiling them in a saucepan.

What are the terrible twos (toddlers at age 2 yr. old)?

Your breasts after baby stops nursing cold turkey.

What is the best time to wean (stop) the baby from nursing?

When you see teeth marks or when dad wants mom's breast for himself only.

What is the grasp reflex (ability of newborn at birth to grasp things tightly)?

The reaction of new father's when he sees new mother's breasts.

Can a mother get pregnant while nursing?

Yes, but it's much easier if she removes the baby from her breast and puts him to sleep first.

Where is the best place to store breast milk?

In your breasts.

What happens to disposable diapers after they're thrown away?

They are stored in a silo in the Midwest, in the event of global chemical warfare.

Why should dim lights be used during homebirth?

Baby wants the same environment as much as possible as inside mom's belly.

Do I have to have a baby shower (party for mom before the baby arrives)?

Not if you change the baby's diaper very quickly.

Why did the newborn stopped cyring during circumcision?

He lost the sense of trust around him after cyring for pain and nobody cared.

What causes baby blues (mild postpartum depression after birth)?

Tanned, hard-bodied bimbos.

Nannies aren't cheap are they? Not usually, but occasionally you'll find a floozy.

What is colic (baby crying intensely)? A reminder for new parents to use birth control.

Why is mom lying on her back when in labor which counters gravity? For doctor's convenience.

Why does it take a long time for baby to be delivered when mom is flat on the bed?

Baby has to climb a hill before coming out.

What are night terrors? Frightening episodes in which the new mother dreams she's pregnant again.

Our baby was born last week. When will my wife begin to feel and act normal again?

When the kids are in college.

My childbirth instructor says it's not pain I'll feel during labor, but pressure (muscles and ligaments tightening up to push baby out). Is she right?

Yes, in the same way that a tornado might be called an air current.

WHEN MEMBRANES RUPTURE PREMATURELY (BEFORE 36 WEEKS)

Call your doctor or midwife. They will want to: document that your membranes have ruptured and that the baby's heart rate is okay and do a vaginal culture to rule out GBS or Bacterial Vaginosis, or another infection that could harm you and your baby. Mom should document baby's movement every two hours.

Maintain proper hygiene. It is critically important to avoid infection once the water sac around the baby has broken. That includes avoiding any digital exam as possible (checking the cervix using the gloved fingers).

Take Vitamin C and Echinacea tincture to strengthen the membranes containing amniotic fluid. This would be beneficial when you want the baby to stay longer in your womb and prevent premature labor.

Check temperature hourly and call the doctor or midwife when temperature is above normal (>99) and when accompanied by chills, fever or other sign of infection.

Do not take a bath but shower is ok. Sexual intercourse is avoided.

Get lots of walk, fresh air, and rest well for the coming labor needs lots of your energy.

See Also:

Labor

Birth Plan

Notes: Sometimes you do not need a birth plan. Selecting the doctor or midwife that you can communicate well is important. Remember that hospital protocols and personnel can influence the management of your birth. Be alert to sense when things are not going the way you expect things to happen. The best birth plans and management come with lots of preparation, education, and responsibilities.

Some mothers would present a detailed plan to thier caregivers during one of their prenatals. The nursing staff do not need to know the details but communicate to them in a way that you can express concern while asking for some time before they perform the procedure or an explanation of risks and benefits.

It is best to use the birth plan as your own guidelines as communicated to your partner and your doula. While you are focusing on the birth, your partner and doula can be the advocate or communicator of your wishes. I would not personally present a written plan but I will try to show rapport and cooperation with the nursing staff. The birth plan listed below is for the doctor and not the nursing staff.

We are well prepared and educated for birth. We have done all we can to be healthy and low risk throughout this pregnancy. We have carefully selected each member of our birth team and respect their expert training, and also that of the staff at your hospital. In the light of our thorough preparation, we look forward to this birth being natural and peaceful and will welcome all assistance to that end. We do reserve the right to refuse any medical procedures or drugs which after careful consideration, do not seem appropriate, necessary, or beneficial for the safe and natural unmedicated birth of our child.

We recognize that labor is real work and can be quite lengthy. We expect to work with the contractions and experience all the associated sensations. We plan to walk about, change positions, utilize relaxation and gravity to facilitate its natural progression. We do not anticipate the need for any medications or procedures for labor augmentation or pain relief. We plan to use massage, warm compresses, and herbs for pain relief.

We request that all fetal heart tones be monitored manually and vaginal exams be done minimally when necessary. To minimize the risk of infection, exams should not be performed once the membranes have been ruptured.

As we have no prior history of complications, and plan to drink plenty of clear fluids throughout labor for hydration, we do not anticipate the need for any intravenous devices.

When the pushing stage begins, we plan to utilize upright positions necessary to effectively work with the contractions. We have prepared the perineum for birth, and with proper support and massage, an episiotomy (by the doctor) should not be required. In the event of a tear, the repair may be performed using local anesthesia only after the cord has been cut.

We also recognize that pushing may require several hours. We are prepared to patiently work with the contractions rather than use vacuum extraction or other means solely for the purpose of speeding things up a bit. We request that the baby be lifted to the mother's breast for warming, bonding and sucking immediately following birth. It is our desire to discover for ourselves the baby's gender, rather than be informed by our attendants, after waiting so long for this delightful moment.

After the birth, and once the placenta has been naturally expelled by the mother, we wish for the father to cut the cord. We desire that the baby remain with the mother at all times to be warmed, suckled and bonded with. We request that all procedures and routines such as weighing, measuring, exams, eye drops (delayed for two hours), baths, etc., be done at bedside, or delayed until the mother can accompany the baby elsewhere in the hospital.

Thank you for your help and cooperation with our birth.

Weight Gain Gain weight for the baby (see Preterm birth) by eating quality food. Remember mom needs all the energy later on so eat healthy. Eat small quantities if you like to control your weight but eat at least every two to three hours especially during the last trimester.

Talk to your midwife or doctor about your weight and eating habits. Maintaining a healthy diet leads to easy birth and healthy baby. Do avoid toxins from the environment, plastics, air/water pollution and many hidden toxins.

Avoid crustaceans, cat feces and pools. Do lots of walking but rest a lot too since many sales jobs that require 8 hours of standing predisposes pregnant women to early birth or premature birth in the absence of proper nutrition and prenatal.

Breastfeeding

Most mothers around the world agree that:
The mother's heartbeat is the baby's lullaby music.
The mother's breastmilk has sleep inducing benefits.
The mother's breast is not dropable like a bottle and is easy to carry around.
The mother's breast milk stores the baby's milk at just the right temperature.
The mother's breast milk is readily available any time the baby sucks or cries.
The mother's breast milk stays in a sterile place and stays warm.
The mother's breasts do not need sterilizing, boiling or cleaning with soap (for nipples).
The mother's breasts size does not matter since they always produce the right amount of milk for her baby.
The mother's breasts only absolutely need to be suckled by the baby.
The mother's breast milk makes traveling easy for both baby and mom.
The mother's breast appears pleasing in a natural way to dad's eyes when nursing the baby.
The mother's breast provides the comfort the baby needs when tired, hungry or sick.
The many benefits of breastmilk for mothers and babies include:
Phosphorous which is important for brain growth and development.
Antibodies that will protect the baby against invading organisms.
The effect of a natural vaccine without the risk of artificial vaccines.
Being always in the right formulation with the baby's age.
The absence of allergens.
Comforting the baby's stomach rather than disturbing it.
More iron and other nutrients that are readily absorbed by the baby.
We can tell our partners and friends why we breastfeed our babies. The following sentences reaffirm our commitment to breastfeed our babies:
Breastfeeding is the mother's gift only the mother can give.
Breastfeeding helps make more loving and caring children.
Breastfeeding is the most human form of feeding.
Breastfeeding makese it easier to discipline children.

Breastfeeding is nature's way of helping mom be in love with her baby.

Breastfeeding makes dad happy when seeing his wife and baby nourishing each other.

Breastfeeding helps remove mother's worries for the day.

Breastfeeding increases opportunity for the baby to be massaged by the mother.

Breastfeeding helps mom know her child's growth and developmental changes better.

Breastfeeding helps bring greater rewards for the future generation.

Right Start Breastfeeding Tips

Prepare your nipples, eat well, and sleep when your newborn is sleeping.

Maintain a healthy diet with four fresh vegetables and three kinds of fruits a day. Drink lots of water or juices. A hot soup or soupy dish rich in sea foods and grains is important.

Put your babies to your breast as soon after they are born as possible.

Seek the support of mothers who have breastfed their babies. If breast engorgement occurs: apply warm compress, soak your breast in warm water, make sure that the baby empties your breasts, and follow proper positioning and latching on as instructed by your midwife (see Breastfeeding problems).

Breastfeeding More than one Baby

If you have twins, you are doubly committed to the task of breastfeeding. Your partner is an important resource in giving you time to breastfeed both your babies at the same time or one at a time. Since most twins are premature and tend to be sleepy, not sucking well for the first couple of weeks, a lactation counselor or consultant can help you with the proper latch-on techniques. Get the right start breastfeeding tips before sore nipples or milk supply problems occur. Research has shown that mothers who breastfeed twins simultaneously have higher elevations of the mothering hormone prolactin than those who nurse one baby at a time.

Mother's needs: The needs of a mother are increased with each child to breastfeed so a recommended 3,000 cal/day and increased fluid intake are necessary to maintain the proper nutrition of the mother. Rest is important and support from family and friends can do a great deal in the success of breastfeeding twins or multiples.

Baby's needs: If one of the babies is less demanding, wake that baby up for simultaneous feeding with the hungrier baby during the day. Breastfeed him or her during the night to allow greater weight gain.

For Breastfeeding Positions for Twins, ask your midwife, breastfeeding consultant or childbirth educator (Authors):

Double clutch hold

Cross-cradle position

Parallel position: One baby is in the cradle hold and one is in the clutch hold with their bodies lying in the same direction.

The Family sleeping together helps the baby slowly adjust to his or her environment.

My second child shared bed with us until he was three years of age.

I can feel the contrasting differences between him and his brother who did not shared bed with us. He is so loving to me and we know each other's feelings. He was so attached to me that he cried when I left him and his brother for work abroad. Nurse, mother of two, Philippines

Sharing bed is an old tradition in the Far East. By necessity, a big family of six children shares bed usually on the floor with a mat. Until the children reach the age of about five or six years old.

See also:

Kegel Exercises

Learn to exercise the muscles in your perineum, a sling of muscles that provide support necessary during labor and birth. Tighten these muscles just as you would if you wished to stop the flow of your urine. You can do this anywhere and should be done regularly.

Another way to tone these muscles is through perineal massage where your two fingers or your partner's fingers massage the lower vaginal opening spreading it slowly and downward. Ask your midwife how this should be done.

See also:

Babies

My First Birth with Midwives Assisting

Baby Dominic was born at 6:04am on July 18, 1994. The night before was a Sunday, I decided not to attend 7 pm mass as usual, but to have my husband take me to visit our primary midwife, Saraswathi instead. We visited Saraswathi in Palo Alto at 8 PM. Sara's orders were to find iron supplements, go home, take a warm bath, eat a full meal, drink a glass of wine and go to bed. Later Saras called us at home and discovered we had not done all of those things yet. We had stopped at Country Sun natural foods store and found they didn't have the brand of chelated iron supplements Saras had recommended. There was difficulty finding a suitable substitute, but we finally found it. Then we decided to stop for take out food to bring home to save time.

I waited patiently in the car while my husband got the food and then finally we drove home. My patience was tried again while my husband scrubbed out the bath tub in preparation for my bath. Finally after the meal and the bath and the iron and the wine we got into the bed. But my labor had begun, this being between 10 and 11 PM.

I assumed a position of all fours on my knees on the bed. I began breathing, vocalization and visualization exercises. My husband made his best argument for granting him allowance to sleep but I rejected it. He voiced stubborn expressions of doubts and skepticism. I switched into "override husband" mode, told him to hush up and follow my instructions. The first thing was for him to apply pressure to my lower back. I leaked and we turned on the light to see what color the fluid was. We saw nothing and perhaps we should have realized that being clear it was my watery fluid - not urine. I began moaning and new contractions. At 1:30 am my contractions were lasting about thirty seconds. By 1:45 am they were lasting fifty-five seconds. By 1:50 am they were lasting about ninety seconds.

I was doing a lot of concentrating and listening to the messages from my body. Between 2 and 3 am I decided we should call Saraswathi and ask her to please come and attend. Saras promised to come over fully equipped and to bring her seven month old daughter Sophia.

She informs us that her friend Joanne, a nurse-midwife from Los Gatos, would also be coming to attend.

I remained at my favored all fours position on the bed and instructed my husband to continue hand pressure on my lower back. I visit the toilet, nothing comes out but I vomit up all my supper. We made a second call to Saraswathi because during the first Saras instructed my husband to follow my wishes and to call back if I seemed to be growing delirious with the intensifying level of pain. Saras recommended a heating pad to my lower back but we only had a hot water bottle handy. Saras said to use this as a compress and to call her right back if my situation intensified.

I took at least three separate showers to lessen the pain as Yelena, one of the midwife partners of Saras, had advised in our childbirth preparation class. My husband was trying to fight off waves of sleep and sleep deprivation pangs. I found some pain relief by sitting on the toilet. I complained numerous times of feeling as if I had to go but nothing would come out. My husband gave his speech that maybe I should have drank prune juice blah blah blah. I told him to hush up and come back to holding the hot compress on my lower back while I was on all fours up on the bed. Then at one decisive moment I asked him to call Saras again and ask her to please come right over. Saras responded and soon arrived with baby Sophia and Joanne around 4 am.

As my labor continued, Saras and Joanne started getting things set up. Baby Sophia was placed in the second bedroom with the door closed. I was accomplishing advanced vocalizations and visualization backed up with serious continuous prayer. Saras urged me to mind my breathing to keep better focus and concentration.

Joanne and Saras had various items positioned around the bedroom. We had most of the recommended things on hand, but half of them were in the second bedroom. We were insufficiently prepared to the extent that we had assumed that the delivery was still a week or two off. I was still working in the office that Friday. Later we discovered there was hardly any gas in the tank of our Subaru. There were numerous failures of supporting equipment. The oxygen tank the midwives brought had accidentally leaked, which Joanne noticed and fixed. The flashlights we readied did not operate dependably and at one point my husband had to hold up a table lamp to illuminate me for the midwives. The midwives couldn't find the desired size needle to sew stitches for me. These minor screw-ups were barely noticeable to me, for I was concentrating fully on my laboring. Using all my knowledge and will power I ignored the side events and focused on the main event. I was imagining that my body is opening up. I was seeing beautiful faces of babies with angel-like smiles, mothers holding their babies and nursing them, my baby trying to squeeze out of my birth canal. I was focusing on my breathing for I was aware that my baby was breathing through my breathing.

Saras announced that we would have our baby born within 24 hours and this really woke my husband up! He used all his ability to compress my lower back as I instructed him. My moaning became louder and louder. I was amazed days later when the neighbors claimed they didn't hear anything unusual. I focused on my vocalizations to help my vagina open as fast as I could. I used all the octaves, high, low and in-between. At one point baby Sophia woke up and Saras brought her into the room with us. I appreciated baby Sophia's presence and gained spirit by watching her smile at us from the corner.

Finally my pushing became more and more perfect. While keeping pressure on my lower back, my husband could lean back and see the first image of a tip of a hairy head trying to press out of my vagina. At first just a little sliver of hairy head was visible as the midwives called his attention to it. He could see a little portion of hairy baby head emerge far outside only to disappear back inside my body.

My steady progress was unabated and undeniable. I was incredibly determined to succeed and successfully fought back second thoughts. I know that fear would halt the progress of my labor. I summoned all my will power and my faith that all mothers were designed to labor and birth using the wisdom of their bodies. The stage was there all set for me but I also wondered if it really was possible for my body to withstand the pain and accomplish the birth. I can hear the nurse midwives guiding and coaching me with their suggestions and praises.

The midwives decided to maneuver me off the bed and try for a better position. They had my husband sit in an upright hard-backed chair and I assumed my most comfortable standing squatting position while leaning my back toward my husband. He held me up as I dug my elbows and forearms into his lap. With four pushes, Saras handed the baby to my arms. And as I feel the baby's bottom I shouted 'His a boy.' I shouted ' I love you baby' many times, reassuring my baby that he is welcomed with joy and warmth and that mommy is nearby. My midwife told me to push my placenta out and I did and then she told me to tell my body to stop the bleeding which I did.

My husband was so awestruck that I had to repeat Saras instructions to him that he should cut the cord and so he did. The midwives had wasted no time in presenting our baby in the right position for him to snip the beautiful blue cord with sharp scissors.

I was hugging the baby, looking at his dark eyes and we were communicating to each other without words. I remember I shed a cupful of tears, for it reminded me of the labor for all the mothers in the world and most especially my mother whom I love. My husband felt the joy in my cries and I noticed tears were also flowing from his eyes. He climbed onto the bed on his belly and reached for the baby and me.

My husband and I agreed later that the successful homebirth of our precious baby Dominic was the greatest thing that had ever happened to either of us. The morning baby Dominic was born his father and I basked in the joy and wonder of his arrival. We were filled with respect and gratitude for Saras and Joanne. By 10:00 am, shortly thereafter the midwives and Sophia all left and only my husband, baby Dominc and I were left. There we lay on our bed in peace and joy, despite our exhaustion. Seemingly for hours we simply stared in loving admiration at our newborn baby.

Herbs and Nutrition
Eat for You and for Your Baby

Your baby is nourished by your body as the plant obtains nourishment from the soil. A healthy baby is the result of a healthy mother. It is good to know which of the foods that we take contribute to a healthy baby. Most herbs listed here (except for the red raspberry) should be taken during the last trimester and only after consultation first with your midwife or doctor.

Carbohydrates

Each gram of carbohydrates provides the body with four calories. Most foods containing carbohydrates have other essential nutrients such as honey and blackstrap molasses which also contain iron and B vitamins. Grains, fruits and vegetables contain carbohydrates which provide fuel and energy for the body. Pregnant mothers need about 2,200 calories per day while nursing mothers need these and an additional of about 800 calories per day.

Proteins

Many a pregnancy induced hypertension could be avoided by taking an adequate amount of protein. About 90 grams of protein is needed by a pregnant mother for the growth and maintenance of body tissues of the baby and the mother. Complete protein foods are found in meat, fish, eggs, milk and cheese while incomplete protein foods are found in legumes, grains, seeds and nuts. Some sources of protein include: meat, poultry, fish, eggs, milk, nuts, beans, peas. Some combinations of proteins providing the complete protein that the body needs are:

rice and legumes
rice and legumes and wheat
wheat, sesame and soybean
corn and legumes
rice and milk or wheat
peanuts and milk
wheat and legumes

wheat and cheese
wheat and milk

Fats

Your fat intake should be about 35% of your total calories. Each gram of fat provides the body with nine calories. Fat is important in maintaining body heat especially in cold climates. It aids in the absorption and utilization of carotene, the vegetable form of Vitamin A.Vitamins

Vitamin A is essential for good vision. It helps reduce susceptibility to infection. It is essential for healthy skin, good blood, strong bones and teeth, kidneys, bladder, lungs, and membranes. Natural Sources: Fish liver oils, sheep and beef liver, carrots, yams, dairy products, liver, dark green and yellow leafy vegetables.

Beta Carotene provides the body with a safe source of Vitamin A. It works with other natural protectors to defend your cells from harmful free radical damage. Natural Sources: Dark green leafy vegetables, yellow and orange vegetables and fruits.

Vitamin B-1 (Thiamine) aids in digestion. It is necessary for metabolism of sugar and starch to provide energy. It maintains a healthy nervous system. Alcohol can cause deficiencies of this vitamin and all the B-complex vitamins. Natural Sources: Brewer's Yeast, wheat germ, liver, whole-grain cereals, fish and poultry, egg yolks, nuts, legumes, brown rice, and blackstrap molasses.

Vitamin B-2 (Riboflavin) helps the body obtain energy from protein, carbohydrates and fats. It helps maintain good vision and healthy skin. Natural Sources: brewer's yeast, alfalfa, almonds, liver and other organ meats, leafy vegetables, whole-grain breads and milk.

Vitamin B-3 (Niacin) helps the body utilize protein, fats and carbohydrates. It is necessary for healthy nervous system and digestive system. Natural Sources: lean meats, poultry, fish, peanuts, milk and milk products, and rice bran.

Vitamin B-5 (Panthothenic Acid) helps release energy from protein, carbohydrates and fats. It is needed to support a variety of body functions, including the maintenance of a healthy digestive system. Sources: royal jelly, brewer's yeast, brown rice, organ meats, salmon, egg yolks, legumes, wheat germ.

Vitamin B-6 (Pyridoxine) is essential for the body's utilization of protein. It is needed for the production of red blood cells, nerve tissue and antibodies. Women taking oral contraceptives have lower levels of Vitamin B-6. Drinking alcohol also lowers the level of B-6 in the body. Natural Sources: brewer's yeast, meats, whole grains/wheat, bananas, green leafy vegetables, liver, brown rice, soybeans, rye, and lentils.

Vitamin B-12 (Cyanocobalamin) is necessary for the normal development of red blood cells, and the functioning of cells, particularly in the bone marrow, nervous system and intestines. Natural Sources: meat, sardines, mackerel, dairy products and fermented soy products.

Biotin is important in the metabolism of fats, carbohydrates and proteins. Natural Sources: liver, brewer's yeast, eggs, sardines, legumes, brown rice and whole-grain cereals.

Vitamin C is necessary to produce collagen, the connective material of all body tissues. It is important for healthy teeth and gums. It strengthens capillaries and other blood vessels. It plays an important role in healing injuries. It aids the body's absorption of iron. It helps fights infection and it is important in boosting the immune system. Taken by mothers with breast engorgement, mastitis, or any time the body feels weak.

Vitamin C is water soluble so it cannot be stored by your body and must be frequently replaced. Stress decreases your body's supply of Vitamin C. Clinical tests have shown that smokers and women taking birth control pills have significantly lower blood levels of

Vitamin C than non-smokers and women who are not taking birth control pills. Natural Sources: Citrus fruits and juices, acerola cherries, cantaloupe, broccoli, alfalfa sprouts, tomatoes, green and red peppers, and strawberries.

Choline is an element found in lecithin which is considered important in the transmission of nerve impulses. Natural Sources: lecithin, egg yolks, liver, wheat germ, Brewer's yeast.

Vitamin D is necessary in the absorption of calcium and phosphorous which are required for bone formation. It is also necessary in maintaining a stable nervous system and normal heart function. Take a nice walk and get fresh, clean air daily. Other sources: sardines, salmon, tuna, egg yolk, sunflower seeds.

Vitamin E protects fat soluble vitamins and red blood cells. It is essential in cellular respiration and protection. It inhibits coagulation of blood by preventing clots. Sources: wheat germ, safflower nuts, sunflower seeds, whole wheat.

Minerals

Calcium is the most abundant mineral in the body. It is essential for the formation and repair of bone and teeth. It regulates certain body processes such as normal behavior of nerves, muscle tone and blood clotting. Natural Sources: Milk and milk products, fish and other seafoods, green leafy vegetables, citrus fruits, dried peas and beans. About 800 mg per day are required for a pregnant mother. The following table lists the food sources and amount of calcium in each food.

Food: 200 mg = 3/4 cup baby cereal 185 mg = 1 cup cream of wheat 50 mg = 2 eggs

Fish: 150 mg = 3.5 oz. Canned herring 250 mg = 3.5 oz. Canned mackerel 200 mg = 3.5 oz. Canned salmon with bones 100 mg = 3.5 oz. oysters 350 mg = 3.5 oz. sardines with bones

Cooked Beans: 50 mg = 1/2 cup white 50 mg = 1/2 cup red

40 mg = 1/2 cup limas 75 mg = 1/2 cup soybeans 50 mg = 1/2 cup garbanzos 25 mg = 1/2 cup lentils

Greens: 120 mg = 1/2 cup beet greens 90 mg = 2/3 cup broccoli 60 mg = 1/2 cup chard 150 mg = 1/2 cup collards 90 mg = 1/2 cup kale 140 mg = 1/2 cup mustard greens

Dried fruits: 100 mg = 4 figs 100 mg = 8 prunes

50 mg = 1/2 cup raisins 100 mg = 1 large orange

Nuts: 125 mg = 1/3 cup almond, unblanched 200 mg = 1/3 cup brazil nuts 50 mg = 1/4 cup peanuts with skin 50 mg = 1/4 cup peanut butter 50 mg = 1/2 cup English walnuts

Herbs rich in calcium: amaranth, kelp, parsley

Chromium acts with insulin to enable the body to utilize glucose, the form in which the body utilizes carbohydrates. Natural Sources: Thyme, black pepper, Brewer's yeast, liver, whole wheat and whole-grain cereals.

Copper is active in the storage and release of iron to form hemoglobin for red blood cells. Natural Sources: Organ meats, shellfish, nuts and dried legumes.

Iron

Iron is an essential part of hemoglobin, a protein structure which helps the red blood cells to carry oxygen throughout the body. Iron is important for maintaining blood volumes. About 40 mg per day are required for a pregnant mother. Mother's wisdom tells us to consume three to five times a day of greens, fruits, nuts, and other healthy food during pregnancy. Mothers before us have prepared well during pregnancy thru proper nutrition.

Pregnant moms should consume more iron to compensate for the expansion of plasma volume during the last trimester which leads to decline in the hemoglobin and hematocrit

values in the blood. Iron is important in providing oxygenation for mother and baby. It can mean less bleeding after birth and a healthy baby with no breathing-related problems.

Holistic midwives suggest an iron tonic of yellow dock root made into a tea sweetened with honey. A hot morning drink containing blackstrap molasses sweetened with honey can be a good substitute for coffee drinkers. Cooking in cast iron pans can help in iron absorption.

When cooking try to combined one or two kinds of food with vitamin C-rich food. Nothing beats organic or pesticide-free produce from the farmer's market and also avoid eating canned or processed foods heavily laden with carcinogens or chemical preservatives. Whole-grain foods such as whole wheat flour of almond, rice, or corn of almond, rice, or corn/ bread, brown sugar, unprocessed grains - rolled oats, bulgar wheat, brown rice - contain twenty more nutrients than refined flour of almond, rice, or corn of almond, rice, or corn.

Though absorption of iron in meats is greater than in veggies, vegan moms can still get the necessary amount of iron by eating a wide variety of iron-rich foods.

Iron is important for maintaining blood volumes. About 60 mg of iron per day are required for a pregnant mother due to higher blood volume and the demands of fetus and placenta. The following table lists the food sources and amount of iron in each food.

Sources: 1.3 mg = 1 cup of raw bean sprouts 3.1 mg = 1 tbsp blackstrap molasses 1.1 mg = 2/3 cup broccoli greens 2.5 mg = 3 oz canned sardines 7.5 mg = 3 oz beef liver, sauteed 5.2 mg = 3 oz clams, oysters, other seafoods 2.0 mg = 3 oz chicken 2.8 mg = 1 medium potato baked with skin 1.4 mg = 1 tbsp brewer's yeast 1.0 mg = 1 egg Dried fruits/juices/nuts: 5.1 mg = 10-12 halves apricots 5.1 mg = 10-12 halves peaches 10.5 mg = 8 oz prune juice 5.6 mg = 1 cup raisins 3.8 mg = 3 .5 oz cashew nuts 5.0 mg = 3.5 oz chocolate bittersweet

Cooked Beans/Nuts: 2.1 mg = 1 cup walnuts 13.8 mg = 1 cup red 15.6 mg = 1 cup limas 16.8 mg = 1 cup soybeans 13.8 mg = 1 cup garbanzos 13.6 mg = 1 cup lentils 6.8 mg = 1 cup peanuts roasted with skin 6.4 mg = 1 cup peanuts roasted without skin 15.6 mg = 1 cup white beans 15.4

mg = 1 cup mung beans 10.2 mg = 1 cup common peas 22.4 mg = 1 cup pumpkin and squash kernels 14.2 mg = 1 cup sunflower seed kernels 2.0 mg = 1/2 cup barley

1.5 mg = 1/2 cup kidney Others: 1.9 mg = 2/3 cup beet greens kelp caviar, buckwheat, oats, hazelnuts, wheat germ

Herbs for anemia: alfalfa, clover, dandelion, red raspberry

Note: Oregano inhibits iron absorption.

Folic Acid is used in red blood cell formation. It aids in metabolism of proteins and is necessary for growth and division of body cells. It is an essential vitamin for pregnant women, and deficiencies have been linked with birth defects. Spina Bifida and Anecephaly are two Neural Tube Defects that appear to be preventable with just 400 mcg of folic acid. Folic Acid is considered brain food, and is needed for energy production and the formation of red blood cells. It functions as a co-enzyme in DNA and RNA synthesis. It is important for healthy cell division and replication. In pregnancy it helps regulate embryonic and fetal nerve cells formation, which is vital for normal developmnent. To be effective in prevention, this nutrient must begin before conception, and continue well into the pregnancy. Folic acid works best when combined with Vitamins B12 and C. Good sources are: brewer's yeast, alfalfa, endive, chickpeas, oats, enriched cereals, fruits and fruit juices, leafy green vegetables, barley, beef, bran, brown rice, cheese, liver, milk, mushrooms,salmon, tuna, wheat germ, whole grains, and whole wheat.

Iodine sources: Kelp, cod liver oil

Magnesium helps in the absorption and use of calcium and phosphorous. It aids in bone growth and is necessary for proper functioning of nerves and muscles. Natural Sources: Green vegetables, seeds, nuts and whole grains.

Manganese is needed for normal tendon and bone structure. Natural Sources: bran, cloves, ginger, buckwheat, oats, hazelnuts, chestnuts, tea leaves, peas and beans.

Potassium is a mineral found in the cell fluid throughout the body. It helps regulate your body's water balance. It is necessary for normal growth and muscle function. Natural Sources: Green leafy vegetables, oranges, whole grains, potatoes (with skin), broccolie, avocado, brussels sprouts, cauliflower, cantaloupes, dates, prunes and bananas.

Selenium works with Vitamin E. Natural Sources: bran, broccoli, onions, tomatoes, tuna, corn, cabbage, whole wheat, beans and wheat germ.

Zinc is essential for growth, tissue repair and sexual development. Sources: herring, sesame seeds

More about Herbs

General Toner Herbs: Red raspberry, squaw vine, crampbark, wild yam (not to be taken during the first and second trimester because of the possibility of fetal masculinization)

Pre-eclampsia or Pregnancy-induced Hypertension Herbal Helpers: alfalfa, dandelion, peppermint, parsley

Labor Herbal Helpers

Note: Most labor herbal helpers should not be used during pregnancy except during labor.

To cleanse the birthing place: cedar, sweetgrass, sage, lavender, rosemary

To ease labor pains: squaw vine, *blue cohosh (not to be used with women with heart disease), bethroot (or birthroot is used by the Native Americans to reduce postpartum bleeding), lavender essential oil (causes anticonvulsant activity and sedative effects), bay laurel, lemon balm, celery, valerian essential oil (aromatheraphy for its sedative effect), wild yam

*Note: Blue Cohosh is an agent to induce labor. It contains glycoside which stimulates smooth muscle in the uterus. It is not to be used in clients with heart disease.

To stimulate labor or increase contractions: blue cohosh, penny royal oil, rue, tansy, skullcap, motherwort, angelica

To relax labor or decrease contractions: lobelia, celery, valerian, chamomile, lemon balm

To expel placenta: angelica, penny royal, chamomile, basil, licorice (contains oxytocin), blue cohosh

To stop hemorrhage: cayenne, shepperd's purse, motherwort, blue cohosh, bethroot, angelica, licorice, comfrey, saffron

Store Up Energy for Birth

Mothers can take a pointer from the way runners prepare for a marathon to ease birth. Load up certain foods so you will store up needed energy for delivery:

Eat meals rich in complex carbohydrates such as pasta.

Take in more potassium (figs, bananas, legumes, lean meat) to help release energy from protein, fats, and carbohydrates.

Have extra helpings of citrus fruit and juice and iron-rich foods.

During delivery, you will lose a certain amount of Vitamin C, which is needed for the healing process after birth. Iron will give you the needed strength.

What to avoid?

Preservatives such as nitrates, Red 40, BHA, BHT etc.

Caffeine, alcohol, too much salt and refined sugar

Your needs and expectations

Having a baby is a profound passage in a woman's life. As an expectant mother you are endowed with the power to bear a child and participate in the creation of a new life. Together with your partner, you will traverse a most satisfying event as you master the birthing of a new life. Pregnancy allows you to examine the world around you more closely.

Take care of yourself

You are now more sensitive to the things around you as you are entering a sacred life experience. With empowerment and joyful feelings, you can surrender to the work of creation. This birth is special for you.

REFERENCE:

Complimentary and Alternative Medicines - Charles Feltrow, PharmD and Juan Avila, PharmD. It is available from Springhouse Corporation, 1111 Bethlehem Pike, P.O. Box 908, Springhouse, PA 19477.

Encyclopedia of Natural Medicine by Michael Murray

Prescriptions for Natural Healing by James Balch.

March of Dimes http://www.modimes.org/Programs2/FolicAcid/Default.htm

Herbal Agents Resource List

American Botanical Council http://www.herbs.org

APRALERT http://www.pmmp.uic.edu

The Australasian College of Herbal Studies http://www.achs@herbed.com

Center for Disease Control and Prevention http://www.cdc.gov

Lloyd Library http://www.libraries.uc.edu/lloyd

Office of Dietary Supplements National Institute of Health http://www.odp.od.nih.gov

Office of Alternative Medicine http://www.altmed.od.nih.gov

US Food and Drug Administration http://www.fda.gov

US National Library of Medicine http://www.nlm.nih.gov

IMAGINE A MOTHER

Imagine a mother who believes it is blessed to be pregnant. A mother who feels the divine work of love in her womb. A mother who is conscious of choices about her pregnancy. A mother who nurtures the life inside her body with natural nourishment for body and soul. A mother who listens to the wisdom of her body and senses all the life force inside her womb.

Imagine a mother who believes she is designed to give birth. A mother who trusts and respects her body. Who listens to her needs, urges to push or bear down the coming baby. A mother who meets these bodily changes and life force with courage and wisdom.

Imagine a mother who has acknowledged the wisdom of mothers before her. A mother who has lived through the past. Who has healed into the present.

Imagine a mother who decides her own labor and birth. A mother who trusts in her ability to give birth. Who refuses to surrender her body and baby to unnecessary medical interventions.

Imagine a mother who knows where to birth her baby. A mother who is not subjected to fear of childbirth but empowered by the life giving force it brings. A mother who seeks other mothers and her partner for support. A mother who takes care of her body and her baby's nutrition. A mother who believes in the successful work of nature. A mother who bonds with her child from conception onwards. A mother who grows in love as she carries the life within her to the world.

ABOUT THE AUTHOR

Connie was born and raised in the Philippines. She is the eldest of the family of 6. At age 19,she has to support her family by working as a high school science and math teacher, while still completing her BS in math, minor in chemistry. She then worked at Intel and Acer and later on in various bay area biotech and medical device companies.

She has two children born at home with midwives. During the first three years of their lives, she stayed home and studied midwifery and nursing, home study. She went back to work after three years since the bay area standard of living is high and housing/day care is expensive.

She also worked for less than a year as a pharmacy technician instructor and always reminded her students the side effects of neuro meds and most medicines.

She was told by one bay area school where she wanted to be a certified Nurse Midwife that she cannot enrol with 2 young children and without writing a book. She then wrote an ebook, Birthing Ways Healing Ways, a holistic childbirth ebook.

In the bay area, she moved from one biotech to medical device companies and then she started her home care organization agency in 2018 to help families with finding caregivers and caring for their home-bound loved ones who had Alzheimers, cancer, Parkinsons and other chronic health diseases.

Since 2000, she has been helping caregivers working in care homes including her mother, who was a caregiver for 18 years by driving them and helping out. She learned about senior care and care homes and had an RCFE administrator license but has no house to open a care home business. She also had worked as a caregiver when in between jobs for the last six years and learned about cancer and death.

Printed in the United States
By Bookmasters